SAN MATEO!

A Sketchbook Tour
of the San Francisco Peninsula's Past

Ken Paul
Alexandra Gautraud

CastleRock Press
Palo Alto, California

Published by CastleRock Publishing, 4090 Ben Lomond, Palo Alto, CA 94306.

Library of Congress Cataloging-in-Publication Data

Paul, Ken.
    San Mateo! : a sketchbook tour of the San Francisco
Peninsula's past.

    Bibliography: p.
    1. San Mateo County (Calif.)--History, Local.
2. San Mateo County (Calif.) in art.   3. Historic
buildings--California--San Mateo County--Guide-books.
4. San Mateo County (Calif)--Description and travel--
Tours. I. Gautraud, Alexandra. II. Title.
F868.S19P38 1988   979.4'69   88-30003
ISBN 0-944879-03-9

Contents

Foreword

The noted nineteenth century historian William H. Prescott once observed that from a physical standpoint the "surest test of the civilization of a people" was to be found in their architecture, which not only displayed the grand and beautiful, but also demonstrated their handling of the more utilitarian and essential aspects of life and work. In San Mateo County one finds a wide variety of landmarks, veritable footprints in the sands of time, which provide an insight into the life and history of an earlier time.

In this book artist Ken Paul and travel writer Alexandra Gautraud combine their talents to provide an introduction to many of these unique and significant structures and sites from the Peninsula's colorful past. It is designed as a guide for individuals and families to use in discovering the rich heritage that is around us. It's organization geographically into three divisions—Coastside, Highlands, and Bayshore—easily facilitates touring.

With sensitivity and a sharp eye for detail, Ken Paul captures the essence of structures in sketches which are at once almost photographic and yet impressionistic. Alexandra Gautraud's accompanying text provides helpful driving directions to each location and a lively background narrative.

With these two as our guides, let us tour the Peninsula and drink in its rich history.

Mark S. Still, Ph.D.
Past President, San Mateo County Historical Association
Regional Vice President, Conference of California Historical Studies

Introduction

Have you wondered where San Francisco's major source of water came from in its early days? Where did the lumber come from to build the City's houses? In this book prepare to enter a world of historical structures — a railroad on the coastside, disappearing resorts, homes of the poor and the famous.

It was in the mid-sixties that I began to draw San Francisco's Victorian houses. The drawings were done in a contour style, that is, the eyes tell the hand where to move in a continuous line with an occasional glance at the paper. Some call it "taking a line for a walk." This style of drawing has been used for over twenty years, except the sites have moved from San Francisco to the Peninsula's bay, hills and coastside. This collection of sketches is a dialogue between me, as the artist, and historical structures.

Alexandra Gautraud writes on the unique stories surrounding these structures. Her New England upbringing helps to relate the feelings of the Colonial history in the East Coast to the Wild West structures of the Pacific.

A suggestion to the reader is first to look at the sketches, read a few captions, then choose something of interest to read. This is one way to let the book talk to you and allow your own historical past to unfold in your imagination and memory.

Enjoy the journey!

Ken Paul
November 1988

The Coastline

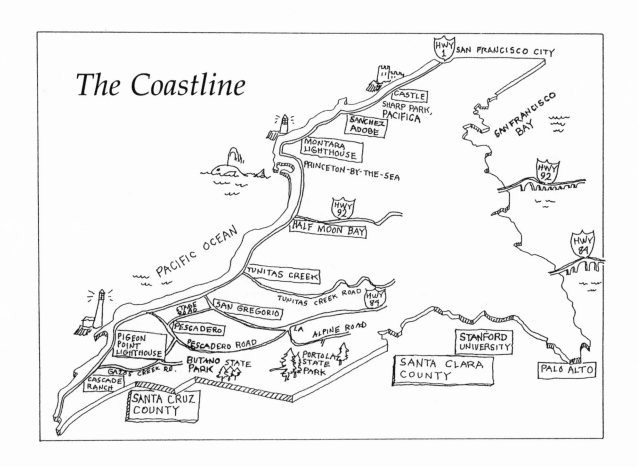

McCloskey's Castle

PACIFICA

We speak of building castles in the air because the real ones seem to float above the landscape. Some brood, some glower while others dominate the scene, but none integrate with their surroundings.

In Pacifica, McCloskey's Castle sits high above the commuter traffic that zips along Highway 1 headed for suburban homes. Built in 1908 by former Congressman ''Pete'' McCloskey's grandfather, it remains an oddity from the early days of this century. Inspired by his wife's native England, this grand home is constructed of large concrete blocks, steel rods for reinforcement, quarried stone, and guarded by gargoyles and griffins.

Today, McCloskey's Castle is a private residence. If you would like to have a closer look at the exterior and gardens, park your car near Oceana High School on Paloma Avenue. Walk up the steep roadway, leading to the summit above Eureka Square and the front entrance to McCloskey's Castle. The figures above the main gate formerly graced the interior of the Fox Theater in San Francisco.

To experience the view from these heights, walk to the end of Mirador Terrace and look toward the ocean. Beyond the traffic of the freeway stretches the old section of Salada Beach as developed by the Ocean Shore Railroad. The municipal pier, always covered with a bevy of fishermen, stretches far into the ocean.

Take Paloma Avenue across Highway 1 to visit some of these special places. But, just before you cross over the freeway take a look at Anderson's Store

A view of the castle from Highway One below a bluff overlooking the ocean.

(320 Paloma Avenue). Once known as Salada Mercantile, this grocery store has been in continuous operation since 1907.

On the ocean side of the highway, The Little Brown Church welcomes visitors. This community church has been at the corner of Francisco Boulevard and Salada Avenue since the early days of Pacifica. This church has served the area since the Ocean Shore Railroad opened these lands to the growing number of people who wanted to spend a day at the beach or a lifetime at the seaside.

Sanchez Adobe

PACIFICA

For the weekend visitor, Pacifica offers ocean beach, surf, and fog. Another side of this community remains hidden beyond the Coast Highway. To explore this other dimension, turn the corner at Linda Mar Boulevard and Highway 1 and persevere past the modern conveniences of the growing suburbs. Shortly, your efforts will be rewarded by the serenity of the Sanchez Adobe.

When Portola's Expedition for Spain arrived in 1769, they found the Ohlones living comfortably along the San Pedro Creek. The oak trees produced large quantities of acorns, small game was easily snared, fish and oysters abounded in the ocean, and the creek ran in every season.

Here on the lee side of Point San Pedro, Don Gaspar de Portola rested his scurvy-ridden troops with the hope that the bountiful land would heal them. During their stay, Portola and his soldiers scaled the heights of a distant ridge to make the wondrous discovery of the San Francisco Bay.

Today, Sweeney Ridge is part of the Golden Gate National Recreation Area and is served by Park Service Rangers who lead walks and present the full picture of the Spanish arrival in the area. The major access to Sweeney Ridge is by car from the west end of Sneath Lane, off Skyline Boulevard in San Bruno. From Sneath Lane it is a one and one-half mile walk to the Portola Discovery Site. From this vantage point visitors have sweeping views of the Pacific coastline,the San Francisco Bay, and the wooded crest of the Santa Cruz Range. For information and a schedule of guided walks, call (415) 556-8371.

Wood pegs are used
to hold together
the large wooden
beams on the Adobe's
porch.

When the Spanish returned in 1775 to establish Mission Dolores in San Francisco, they found the soil and climate there inadequate for their needs. An outpost was established on the adobe site along the banks of the San Pedro Creek. Today, county park officials demonstrate the soil's continuing productivity by maintaining a vegetable garden.

Relax on the broad park benches in front of the adobe. Look at the surrounding hills and the changing skyscape. In the foreground is a variety of trees—rows of pungent eucalyptus, clusters of upright cypress, and a lone twisted cedar.

As you enter the adobe, consider the world of Don Francisco Sanchez. In 1839, Sanchez was granted these two leagues of land but continued to

*A former Ocean
Shore railroad station,
now a private residence,
perched on Pedro Point
in Pacifica.*

live in San Francisco until the completion of his adobe in 1846. Three times
he served as *Alcalde* of San Francisco and today his portrait hangs in the
Gallery of Mayors in City Hall.

Sanchez died on September 8, 1862 at the age of 57 and was buried at
Mission Dolores in San Francisco. He had served under three flags: Spanish,
Mexican, and American.

Step inside the adobe. As you enter the cool interior, time slips from your
shoulders and you find yourself mingling with the remembered figures of
early California before the gold rush changed life forever.

Montara Lighthouse

Montara Lighthouse squats on the bluff overlooking the fog shrouded sea. Constructed in 1875, this miniature version of a grand Victorian lighthouse looks more like a child's playhouse than a beacon for wandering ships.

This treacherous point has seen many shipwrecks. The rocks below the lighthouse hold the last tales of many nineteenth century schooners and tall ships. The first warning device for Point Montara was a steam powered fog signal. In the early 1900s an oil lantern was added along with the Fresnel lens, used to magnify the light. In recent times the light and foghorn have been fully automated.

Vandalism was a recurring problem until the American Youth Hostel established an overnight facility in the Lighthouse Service quarters. In every season the hostel welcomes travelers from around the world.

With volunteer help the American Youth Hostel has restored the keeper's house and struggles to maintain the sheet metal exterior of the lighthouse against corrosion from the salt air. Today the grounds and buildings reflect their Victorian heritage.

The former light station hovers at the brink of the cliff overlooking the rocky shore some 100 feet below. Narrow paths meander through tangy coastal herbs or drop steeply to the mile-long stretch of golden sand that is Montara State Beach.

Surrounded by this tamed wilderness, the hostel's guests are cast into the previous century—to the time when tall ships and heaving schooners rounded this point.

Half Moon Bay

Vasquez House on Main Street.

The artichoke farmer and the pumpkin seeker of the city find the compact town of Half Moon Bay the perfect place for a Saturday afternoon rendezvous. They mingle easily along Main Street. Join them on this historic street and begin your stroll at the old concrete bridge, built in 1900.

Pablo Vasquez, the son of the original land grant holder, established his home at 270 Main. This no-nonsense Greek Revival house stands amid a coastal flower garden. Of special interest are the square Tuscan pillars at the entrance. Its faded yellow exterior with bright blue trim invites speculation about its long history, which began in 1869 when this city was called Spanish Town.

In the 300 block the bright blue building with the lavish garden is an outstanding example of Half Moon Bay's careful preservation of its historic buildings. The Zaballa House was the home of Estanislau Zaballa who in 1863 laid out the Half Moon Bay town site. Today, this structure contains professional offices.

At the corner of Mill Street, the San Benito House and Saloon stands in all its restored glory. The upper floor, its windows decorated with flower boxes, offers bed and breakfast accommodations. The street level boasts a dining room decorated with brass chandeliers. On sunny days the double French doors are opened and guests are served lunch in the garden. This can be a good stop for lunch, dinner, or overnight.

At the principal axis of Main and Kelly Streets, the venerable Cunha Grocery Store entices the visitor to stop and buy some picnic supplies or fresh produce. The interior evokes memories of stores with sweet smelling dried herbs,

Charles Geddes, architect of this church, also designed the Noe Valley Presbyterian Church in San Francisco in 1888, which stands today on Sanchez and 23rd Street.

9

A former railroad depot, now a church social hall.

creaking wooden floors and the aroma of freshly roasted coffee. You can also pick up a compact walking guide to Half Moon Bay at the main counter.

At Miramontes Street, leave Main and head inland toward the hills. On the corner, where Johnston Street meets Miramontes, stands the Methodist Episcopal Church. In 1872 this church was built as a permanent structure for a full time minister.

The congregation, with the help of wealthy land owners, took a major step and asked Charles Geddes, a San Francisco architect, to draw up the plans for their church. Mr. Geddes ornamented the church with moderate touches of the popular Victorian fashion with consideration for the Methodist inherent sense of simplicity.

Perhaps the most ornamented portion of this Gothic Revival church appears in the gabled front entrance. The double doors are topped by a segmented fanlight window and arch. This theme continues along the sides of the building, with each window covered by a simple arch and topped by a cross with a carved letter "M".

The simple bull's-eye window above the door draws attention to the belfry. The use of a Victorian octagonal cupola allows the bell to remain fully visible.

In the 1920s, with the break-up of the Ocean Shore Railroad, the congregation acquired the Half Moon Bay Depot and moved the depot to the rear of the church as a social hall.

As you continue your journey south along the coast, leave the center of town on Main Street to see more of this historic town. Perhaps, the most puzzling set of structures display the bold letters, I.D.E.S. These buildings are the social center of the Portuguese community in Half Moon Bay and home for the Brotherhood of the Holy Spirit, *Irmandade do Espiritu Santo*. This brotherhood is the source of the letters and the biggest festival in town. The festival is sometimes referred to as the Chamarita Festival, which comes from

*Zabella House on Main Street as
seen from the ocean side. It remains
the oldest house in Half Moon Bay.*

Arleta Park Station, a turn-of-the-century railroad depot on Railroad Avenue, now a private residence.

the name of the folk dance performed during the celebration. Parades, pageantry, dancing, and feasting mark this fiesta, which occurs at Pentecost in late May or early June.

Half Moon Bay has come to be recognized for several festivals and celebrations. In early summer a grand rodeo and horse show brings ranchers and city folk together for a week of festivities.

In the fall, people from around the county and Bay Area gather for the great Pumpkin Festival. The fields along the Coast Highway and Highway 92 blossom with round orange pumpkins and with the laughter of children selecting their favorite pumpkin shape for Halloween.

At anytime of the year, Half Moon Bay extends the warmth of a community nestled near the sea and welcomes visitors as a town with a long history of being a way station for the traveler.

James Johnston House

HALF MOON BAY

The James Johnston house, situated on a small knoll along the Higgins Canyon Road, rides the hill like a brilliant summer thunderhead. In springtime, this New England saltbox challenges the lavender wild radishes with the starkness of its shape and the dazzle of its whiteness. This structure makes no attempt to hide its presence or apologize for its existence upon the green hillside.

Late in 1853 James Johnston built this home for his new wife, Petra Maria de Jara. He and his brother, William, planned to establish a dairy farm with the 300 head of cattle that William was driving overland from Ohio.

This was the time before roads connected Spanish Town, as Half Moon Bay was then called, with other communities. The hand-hewn redwood timbers that were used to build the house were brought by ship from Santa Cruz and then floated ashore with the incoming tide.

In building this New England style home, James made a concession to the customs of his California wife. He included a chapel on the second floor.

For six years the house glowed with happiness, parties, and growing children. Then Petra died. James returned to San Francisco and left their three sons to be raised by Petra's mother and unmarried sister. He returned only occasionally to Half Moon Bay.

During the Panic of 1873, James lost most of his holdings and the family was forced to leave their tidy house on the hill. Sometime after this, the house began a steady decline.

Only recently have funds become available to restore the exterior. The City of Half Moon Bay, in cooperation with San Mateo County, has developed plans to fully restore this sentimental reminder of the East Coast. The plans call for complete restoration of the home plus the addition of period furnishings. When the restoration is complete, tours will be given to the public on a regular basis.

Across the road stands a home of the same era, built by James' brother, William. This structure has the flavor of New England with touches of the Victorian period. In building this home wooden pegs were used instead of nails. Today, Westinghouse owns the building and houses farm workers in it.

The Higgins Canyon Road winds through the hillside, passing pastures and farms before entering the steep redwood slopes of the coast range. A short trip along this road makes a pleasant diversion from the flat coastal plain.

This New England style farmhouse can be seen from a distance on Highway 1, south of Half Moon Bay.

WOODEN PEGS USED
TO PUT HOUSE TOGETHER

15

Tunitas Creek

Tunitas Creek was the end of the line for passengers on the Ocean Shore Railroad.

Inland from Tunitas Creek lies the flower fields of the California coast. Small weathered farm houses peek from groves of live oaks pressed by the ocean winds.

An easy back road trip can be made by traveling two miles along Tunitas Creek Road to the junction with Lobitos Creek Cutoff which is on the left and returns to Highway 1 just north of Martin's Beach.

San Gregorio House

San Gregorio House sits on a rise
of land just off the corner of San
Gregorio-La Honda Road and the old
Stage Road. The elongated structure
with a balustrade decorating the second
floor was the nineteenth century answer to
the motel.

The San Gregorio House was built in 1866
on the stage road to Pescadero. Its first owner, George Washington Tully Carter,
firmly believed that San Gregorio, situated along a creek bed, was about to
become a major hub of commercial activity. Carter, the son of a school teacher,
wrote essays for the *San Mateo County Gazette* predicting the future metropolis
at the ocean shore community. It was only a short three years before the
loneliness of the coast began to wear away his enthusiasm.

The hotel changed hands several times and, in 1875, John R. Evans purchased the five acres and small hotel. By this time, San Gregorio showed some
progress toward becoming a thriving community. Down the road a store and

saloon came into operation with a blacksmith shop, butcher store and boot-maker following in short order. The Seaside School and a church rounded out the community.

Evans expanded the existing hotel, which served as a hunter's lodge, and decorated the second floor with the balustrade. In the intervening 110 years, very few changes have been made to the structure.

The original glazing remains in several windows and the four paneled doors are the originals. The color scheme has been changed to brown from the original grey.

In 1888, John Evans sold the inn to Mr. and Mrs. Jesse Palmer, who had worked in the lumbering industry for twenty years prior to the tragic deaths of their four children during a diphtheria epidemic. With this tragedy, they returned to their native England with their surviving daughter. But, the tug of their California home pulled them back to San Gregorio.

Shortly after his purchase, Palmer went into partnership with a local young man, Frank Bell. In time Bell married the Palmers' daughter, Rebecca and, in time, she and her husband operated the inn.

The prospering hotel was self-sufficient, raising their own vegetables and fruits, butchering and curing their own meat, and making all their dairy products. They ran a livery stable with carriages for hire. A dance hall was constructed with a makeshift stage for the orchestra.

By the 1930s, the Coast Highway was completed, and auto traffic speeding south to Santa Cruz bypassed the small town. Business declined rapidly, and Mrs. Bell decided to close the hotel. Today, the San Gregorio House is a private residence for the Bell family. The town has receded to a slower pace. Now, the past is remembered in the tintypes above the bar at Peterson and Alsford's General Merchandise Store and behind the window panes of the San Gregorio House.

San Gregorio Merchandise Store

The name remains the same on the yellowing stucco storefront, Peterson and Alsford, although these owners are long gone from the scene. But, the post office and postmaster are still attached to the store. Everyday at noon the local ranchers stop by for their mail and have a soft drink at the store. Here the latest news about the valley circulates quicker than the bubbles in their drinks.

The San Gregorio Merchandise Store retains the full flavor of a true general store. The large planked floor absorbs all footsteps and the shelves heave with merchandise—enameled pots and pans, milk pitchers, hats, bonnets, old bottles and jars, saddles and saws. It has everything to make this a worthwhile stop for travelers, farmers or sheep herders.

By noon the local gentry gathers at the long bar for sandwiches, coffee, soft drinks, beer or wine. Some gravitate to the oilcloth-covered tables that are surrounded by the wellstocked bookshelves.

Books of every persuasion are sold here—a most remarkable collection of classics, poetry, history, philosophy, guidebooks and nature compendiums. People have lunch with Charles Dickens, Mark Twain, Guy du Maupassant, H. G. Wells and Ghandi. This collection reflects the eclectic interests of the present owners.

On weekends, the general store presents bluegrass and acoustical music with wine and cheese available during the performance. At these times, the atmosphere of the merchandise store is transformed into a cosmopolitan center and the city meets the small town for a brief hour. For information on these performances, call (415) 726-0565.

At the San Gregorio General Merchandise Store, time stands still as if entering the set of an old black and white movie. This is the way the past went shopping on Saturday morning and the news filtered to the farm.

The post office, general store and gas station typify the Three-in-One Country store of many farming communities.

One Room School

SAN GREGORIO

"School days, School days, Yes the Golden Rule days," comes the refrain from the gaslight era. In San Gregorio on a knoll overlooking the Stage Road, these forgotten Golden Rule days can be recaptured for a few moments. There, overlooking the passing pickup trucks loaded with young people headed to Pescadero, stands the Seaside School.

When the school was moved to this site in 1875 by San Mateo County, there were only 75 registered voters in San Gregorio. But these adults show-ed their dedication to education with the building of a one room schoolhouse. The community welcomed the teachers into their homes and lives. Children attended school in the months when harvesting and planting did not demand extra help at home. Heating came from a potbelly stove that the teacher stocked early in the mornings. The two outhouses that provided their primitive sanitation system stand at the rear of the building.

This sturdy building, with the bell tower for calling late students to class, stands as a tribute to the importance of education in San Mateo County from the earliest times.

In 1968 the School District put the building on the auction block; the owners of the surrounding land, which was once part of *Rancho San Gregorio*, were determined to reclaim their holdings. The auction brought some fierce bidding considering the condition and humbleness of the structure. But, Sara and Tom Armstrong of Burlingame succeeded in their bid for ownership and they keep the unoccupied Seaside School in good repair.

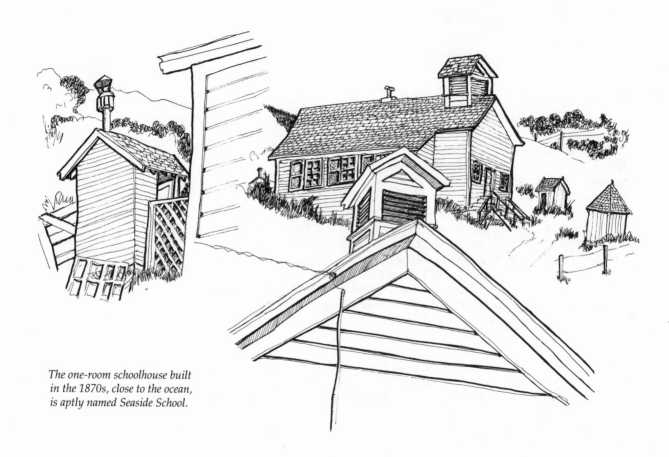

*The one-room schoolhouse built
in the 1870s, close to the ocean,
is aptly named Seaside School.*

Pescadero

Down at Duarte's Tavern they tell the story of the early days of Pescadero when a shipwreck covered the beach with planks of wood and cans of white paint. People carried the bounty back to town, built houses and painted them white.

Duarte's Tavern also began with a good story when, in 1895, Frank Duarte asked a friend to bring a barrel of whiskey from Santa Cruz. When the barrel arrived he set it on a board and started the business that has become today's tavern and restaurant.

Still family operated and open seven days a week, Duarte's is known for ample portions and moderate prices. Their artichoke soup transforms this humble vegetable into a gourmet delight. Some folks say that their olallieberry pie is food for the gods.

More good food can be found across the street at the Arcangeli Grocery where they make sandwiches on their own freshly baked bread. The neat rows of modern shelves conceal the down home butcher's counter that many trendy city markets have tried to duplicate.

For a look at a hardworking general merchandise store try Williamson's General Store. From heavy duty farm equipment to gumdrops for the kids, Williamson's provides the commercial backbone for this one street town.

Town affairs go beyond commercial interests to include church and social gatherings. Near Pescadero Creek on the old Stage Road, the historic Congregational Church sits surrounded by sturdy pines. This church demonstrates the clean lines of Classical Revival form through a semicircular transom, which is used over the door and repeated above the windows along the side of the building. Just below the bell tower, a pseudo-rose window takes the shape of a Maltese cross.

The church appears to have been built of stone but closer examination reveals that the builders scored wood to resemble stone. They intensified this trick-of-the-eye by including the quoins at the corners. Originally built in 1867, the Congregational Church is the oldest Peninsula church still standing on its original site.

Across the Stage Road, the James McCormick house nestles among the willows and alders of the creek bed. The builders of this house also attempted to deceive the eye with scored wood that resembles stone. This 1860s house demonstrates the Classical Revival form in a more sophisticated rendering than other structures in Pescadero.

Just south of the memorial flag on the Stage Road, a group of homes, fraternal organizations, and a church create a historic section within a single block. Grouped along one side of the street the fires spared these structures.

A former Methodist-Episcopal Church now houses the Native Sons and Native Daughters of the Golden West and has not functioned as a church since 1905. The cruciform plan has been mixed with some Gothic Revival details. The facade creates a disturbing unbalanced appearance with the late addition of a smaller lancet window to accommodate a modern restroom. The original construction with redwood timbers explains the continued substantial appearance of this structure.

Once the major center of community activities, the I.O.O.F. Hall now serves as a private residence. Modern additions to this nineteenth century building have removed the classic balance of its planners. The attached garage and mismatched front windows spoil the symmetry of this building. Some semblance of the original design remains with the veranda and balustraded balcony.

The delicate 1890s Woodhams House presents the perfect appearance for a recently married couple. Indeed, the home was built for Alfred Woodhams'

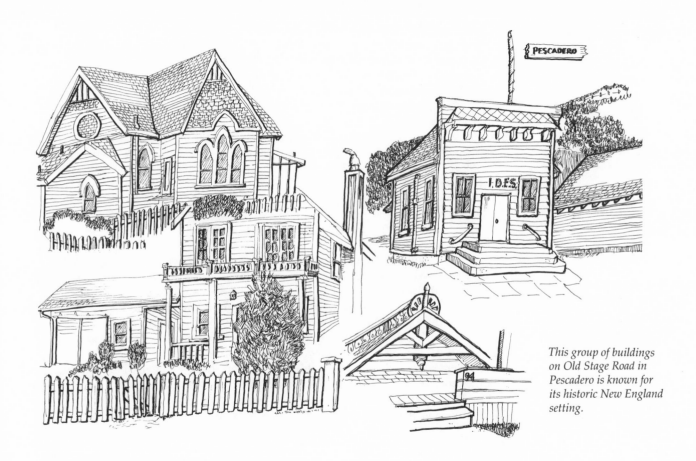

This group of buildings on Old Stage Road in Pescadero is known for its historic New England setting.

bride when the young couple moved to Pescadero to open a butcher shop. The pierced fans at each corner of the porch joined with stick form in the gable combine to create a country-Victorian simplicity.

Last on this very historic block stands a group of buildings with the letters I.D.E.S., which stands for *Irmandade do Espiritu Santo*, Brotherhood of The Holy Spirit, the same as seen in Half Moon Bay. Numerous Portuguese settled in Pescadero and their descendants continue the tradition of the Festival of the Holy Spirit with a parade and barbecue near the time of Pentecost in late May or early June. The town wisely coordinates their celebration with Half Moon Bay to avoid any conflict of schedules. Queens are crowned and join the festivities with the free barbecue.

Other historic buildings spared by the wild fires are located on the far side of town near the cemetery and near North Street. Of special note are St. Anthony's Catholic Church on North Street and the Bartlett V. Weeks house on Goulson Road.

St. Anthony's Church exhibits the same Classical Revival style typified in the town's churches but the spire shows some Gothic influence. During the 1906 earthquake, St. Anthony's was shaken from its foundation and had to be razed. This resulting structure blends well with the architecture of Pescadero.

The third generation of Weeks now occupy the Bartlett V. Weeks house. The appealing front yard garden contains roses, annuals, spring bulbs, and fruit trees. An air of prosperity and care surrounds this home.

This house shows a departure from the older Pescadero homes and demonstrates touches of the Victorian style. The porch posts are not pierced and the double-hung windows have single panes of glass. The original entrance is at the back of the house away from the ocean winds.

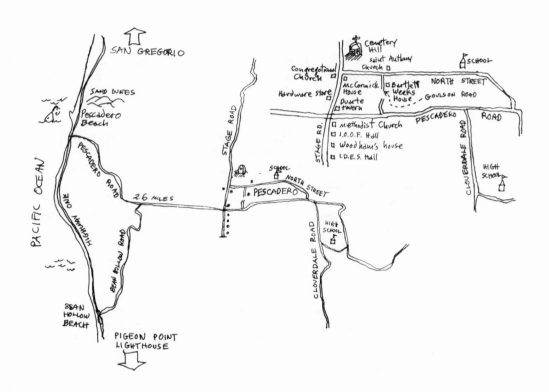

SAN GREGORIO

SAND DUNES

PESCADERO BEACH

PACIFIC OCEAN

PESCADERO ROAD

HIGHWAY ONE

BEAN HOLLOW ROAD

2.6 MILES

BEAN HOLLOW BEACH

PIGEON POINT LIGHTHOUSE

STAGE ROAD

SCHOOL

NORTH STREET

PESCADERO

CLOVERDALE ROAD

HIGH SCHOOL

Cemetery Hill

saint Anthony Church

Congregational Church

SCHOOL

Hardware store

McCormick House

Bartlett Weeks House

NORTH STREET

GOULSON ROAD

Duarte tavern

PESCADERO ROAD

CLOVERDALE ROAD

STAGE RD.

Methodist Church

I.O.O.F. Hall

Woodham's house

I.D.E.S. Hall

HIGH SCHOOL

27

Pigeon Point Lighthouse

As Pescadero and Butano Creeks meet near the ocean, they fan out into an abundant marsh area. The Pescadero Marsh and surrounding 210 acres have been designated a wildlife refuge by the Fish and Game Commission. Here, around two large saltwater ponds, egrets, great blue heron and kites gather.

In the creeks each winter hundreds of steelhead make their spawning run. The numbers today are greatly reduced from the past when fishing attracted sportsmen from San Francisco. The Swanton Hotel sheltered the fishermen and their families for summer vacations. While the men fished, the women and children made the short trip by carriage to Pebble Beach to collect small, sea-polished stones such as jasper, agates, and carnelians.

At Pebble Beach 1.5 miles south of Pescadero the small stones are still knee deep between the sea sculptured cliffs. Today, state park regulations forbid the gathering of pebbles as the supply has become greatly diminished. But, running your fingers through the heaps of stones and sorting for the best color blends can be very relaxing.

For a finer beach surface, Bean Hollow one mile south offers two small but sandy beaches with interesting tide pools near by.

Farther south, about 3.5 miles from Bean Hollow, the Pigeon Point Lighthouse rises majestically from the jutting point. There are no pigeons here. The point was named after the shipwreck of the *Carrier Pigeon* on June 6, 1853.

Before the lighthouse was built, this jut of land, then known as *Punta de la Ballena*, sheltered a community of Portuguese whalers. From this vantage point they watched for migrating gray whales. When the telltale spray marked

When this lighthouse is seen from a distance, the whitewashed bricks merge into a solid shape and color.

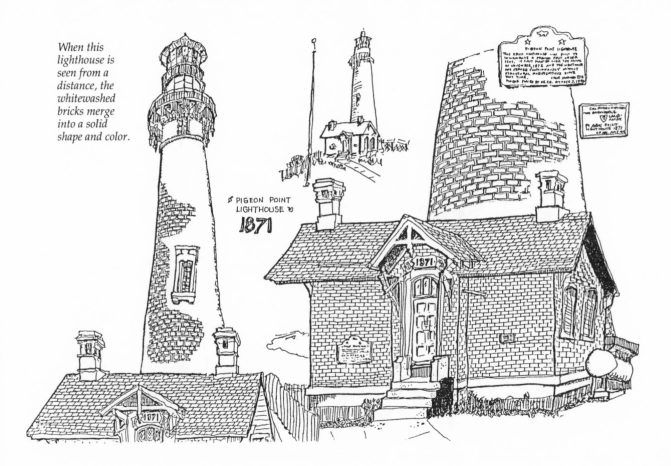

⌐ PIGEON POINT
LIGHTHOUSE ⌐
1871

29

the sky, whalers set out in their whaling boats with rowers, mate and harpooner. When their small vessel was against the whale's body, they drove the harpoon deep into the whale. Now the test consisted of holding onto the creature who, more often than not, won the battle. If the Portuguese whalers judged that they were losing the battle, they cut the Gray whale loose and hoped for better luck with the next one. With the odds against them, this operation did not take a great number of whales. Rather it was the large whaling ships on the open seas that decimated the whale population.

As these Portuguese sailors watched the ocean for whales, they were able to save many shipwrecked crews along this stretch of coast. In the case of the *Carrier Pigeon*, all crew members were brought safely to shore. But the clipper ship, with its gilded, pigeon-shaped figurehead, was lost to the raging sea.

When word reached San Francisco about the *Carrier Pigeon*, the owners dispatched the *Sea Bird* to salvage the *Carrier Pigeon's* cargo before the sea and rocks completed their destruction. As the salvage operation began, the *Sea Bird* floundered in the high seas at the rocky point and this vessel's crew was also rescued by members of the whaling village.

Wrecks along the rocky coastline caused the national Lighthouse Board to consider the establishment of lighthouses along the Pacific shoreline. Alcatraz Island in San Francisco Bay received the first of these beacons. Shortly thereafter, the builder of the Point Reyes Lighthouse, Phineas Marston, received the commission to construct one at Pigeon Point.

Pigeon Point Lighthouse is a brickwork tower with an interior cast iron staircase. Today, this lighthouse is one of the tallest nonreinforced brick structures standing in the United States— somewhat remarkable given the earthquake conditions of the area. Without steel rods or netting of iron wire to bind the bricks and motor, Pigeon Point Lighthouse weathered the 1906 earthquake without cracks or damage.

The light utilized a Fresnel lens from France. Each of the 1,008 prisms were individually molded, hand polished and fitted. The prisms concentrated the light and permitted the use of whale oil and, later, kerosene to produce a strong beam over a great distance. Eventually, electricity replaced these weaker light sources. The original Fresnel lens remains in place although the light was disconnected in 1972.

Through considerable citizen cooperation and combined efforts of several organizations, restoration efforts continue at Pigeon Point Lighthouse. Recently, the steam operated foghorn was refurbished and once again the coastline heard the deep "BeeeeOooooo" of the old diaphones.

The former United States Coast Guard quarters at the base of the beacon provide shelter for travelers as part of the American Youth Hostel system. Small flower gardens surround the low buildings and a white picket fence protects the area from lighthouse visitors.

On weekends, docents lead tours of Pigeon Point Lighthouse, one of the few remaining lighthouses in operation. During the one hour tour, visitors hear tales of the many shipwrecks and enjoy the view from the top of the tower. Call any evening between 5 p.m. and 9 p.m. to make reservations through the American Youth Hostel at Pigeon Point (415) 879-0633 or for information only call the Año Nuevo Interpretive Association (415) 879-0454. A donation is requested for these tours.

Cascade Ranch

Weathered barns, tidy farm houses and rolling pastures remind the traveler of the *Steele Brothers'* vast dairy lands that once covered the coast from Pigeon Point to Año Nuevo State Reserve.

On a spring day in the 1860s, the first Steeles arrived in these lush fields. Years before, the Gold Rush had called them West, but like many others their gold fever transformed into another pursuit.

The *Steele Brothers* dairies had their beginning on the foggy cliffs of Marin County along the Point Reyes seashore. When their lease was about to be terminated in Marin, they brought this special dairy know-how to the San Mateo coast. In time, this business entity operated five dairy ranches, known as *Steele Brothers*, between Gazos Creek and the county boundary.

During the Civil War their patriotism caused them to donate a two-ton cheese for the fund raising efforts of the U.S. Sanitary Commission, the equivalent of today's Red Cross. In the days before refrigeration, cheese was the chief product of these dairies.

The Cascade Ranch remains with its tree-shaded drive and presents an elegant reminder of the great dairying days of the past century. The ranch house is the most elegant of the buildings with a wide veranda and second story balcony along the front and both sides of the house. This home crystallizes the coastal spirit that made the *Steele Brothers* dairy world renowned.

Cascade Ranch. The building on the left was used by Steele Bros. Dairy to make cheeses.

33

1860's

In the 1860s a major production was cheese-making from
the Steele Brother's Cascade Ranch located by Highway 1.

34

Just south of the Cascade Ranch the most interesting natural area along the coast comes into view. The Año Nuevo State Reserve has been established to protect the unusual wildlife of this area. Each year Año Nuevo Point and Island become the site for the mammoth elephant seals' unique mating and birth rituals.

Around Thanksgiving, the male elephant seals, each weighing close to three tons, haul themselves ashore at the Point. During the first two weeks of December male seals with their rumpled noses engage in bloody battles for dominance throughout the dune region. By mid-January the reserve holds more than 1000 seals and in February the number swells close to 1500 with the addition of newborn pups. The scene boggles the imagination with pups, molting adult females, juveniles and yearlings mixed with the bulls whose vocalizations dwarf the other sounds of the rookery.

Reservations for winter tours of the reserve are in high demand. *Ticketron* handles all reservations for the two and half hour docent-led tour, which includes a three-mile walk through the area. Tours are conducted daily from December through April. The area is open only to visitors on tours during this busy season.

At other times of the year the reserve and visitor center are open daily with a per car visitor charge. Even in the off season the air is filled with the barking of seals on Año Nuevo Island. Surfers enjoy the wave action at the point and docents are available for short explanatory walks. A bird checklist for the area is available in the bookstore.

The visitor center is housed in a barn that was once part of *Steele Brothers* and offers a view of dairy farming in the past along with excellent botany displays. Picnic tables are located near the center, within sight and sound of the seashore.

A visit to the Año Nuevo State Reserve represents the San Mateo Coast. Here within a small area of dunes, rocky shoreline and sturdy grasslands, the past and present of the coast coexist with hope and plans for a bright future.

Cascade Ranch House.

36

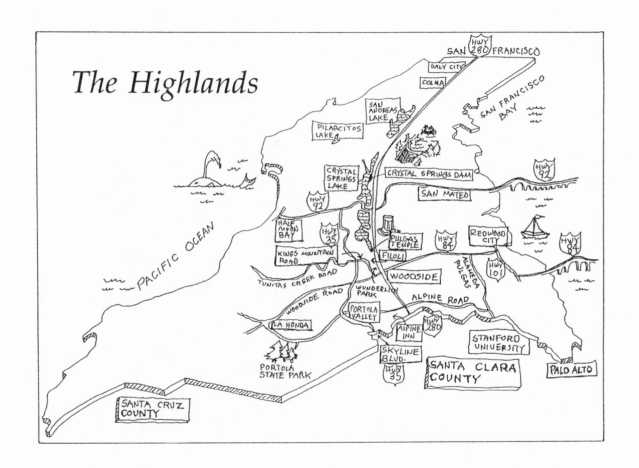

The Highlands

*A house built in 1906,
Daly City.*

Daly City

From the hills overlooking Daly City, the urban scene quickens the pulse of every city dweller. At night the lights of the city tantalize the senses with excitement.

However, at the turn of the century this area possessed a bucolic atmosphere. When the 1906 earthquake struck, John Daly's dairy operated on the hill just outside the San Francisco city limits. To the south were vegetable fields and hog ranches.

Of all the locales on the Peninsula, John Daly's farm felt the greatest impact from fleeing families. He welcomed them to his land, allowed them to pitch their tents, and, in time, sold them patches of land. Although the area looked like any other refugee camp, these people had bought lots and planned to stay.

By 1911 with community needs growing, they voted to incorporate. They selected the name, Daly City, as a tribute to John Daly who had welcomed them to his dairy land in their time of great need.

During the 1930s, WPA writers recorded the view from the hill as still sparsely populated with fields of artichokes, lettuce, brussels sprouts, pansies, marigolds, and violets. At the time the population was a mere 7,838.

This mixture of truck farms and homes came to a sudden conclusion with the post-war boom. Daly City grew by leaps and bounds and annexed surrounding hills and valleys. Today this rapid expansion has eased.

The heart of Daly City's activity is the neo-classical civic center which was designed by architect Donald F. Haines. Completed in 1967, this collection of government units stands on 90th Street between Edgeworth and Sullivan Avenues. As part of the city hall, an art gallery is located on the third level. The Daly City History Arts Guild selects the art for the exhibit which is changed monthly. The gallery is open during office hours Monday - Friday from 8:30 a.m. to 4:30 p.m. On weekends visitors can enter the gallery through police headquarters in the civic center.

Another well known structure in Daly City is the Cow Palace on Geneva Avenue near Bayshore Boulevard. This immense reinforced concrete arena was built in 1936 from a design by W. D. Peugh as the State Livestock Exhibit Pavilion. The arena measures 142 feet by 257 feet. Over the years the walls have reverberated with the sounds of rodeo crowds, circus performances, college and professional basketball games, hockey teams, major prize fights, and the 1964 Republican National Convention.

Today Daly City is the second most populous city in the county, just behind San Mateo. Also, it was rated by the Association of American Geographers as the second most ethnically diverse city in the United States.

Cow Palace, Daly City.

Cemetery City

COLMA

Some residents of Colma are known for their silence. For them, Colma is Cemetery City, and only the rustle of giant eucalyptus trees breaks the peace of the dead.

Today Colma, a thriving community, is both home and workplace for more than 750 lively concerned citizens. Gone are the days when the cemeteries controlled the inner workings of city hall government. Almost forgotten is the time in 1924 when the cemetery owners decided to mark off their boundaries and to include very carefully the necessary 500 residents for incorporation under California law.

In their haste to incorporate, these businessmen selected the name Lawndale, which held a special cemetery ring and an artificial calm. However, after incorporation, the founders discovered that they could not have a post office. The postal service informed them that there already was a Lawndale, California. So, from 1924 to 1941 they operated under the curious condition that although their city did not have a post office, the nearest post office, Colma, did not have a city! So, by a simple election in 1941, Lawndale changed its name to Colma and, thus, acquired a post office.

Every faith and denomination is represented within the borders of Colma's cemeteries. The oldest cemetery is Holy Cross, which was founded in 1887 and continues to accept burials from the San Francisco Catholic Archdiocese. In 1889, two Jewish cemeteries opened: Home of Peace and Hills of Eternity. In 1892, Cypress Lawn was established and, in 1896, Mount Olivet. The Italian Cemetery followed in 1899.

The oldest cemetary is Holy Cross Cemetary founded in 1887.

41

Colma's Town Hall is at the foot of Serramonte Boulevard, also known as Automobile Row.

Legislation in San Francisco caused this burst of cemeteries just beyond the city's boundaries. Pressed by the demands for more land, the San Francisco Board of Supervisors passed an ordinance prohibiting burials in the City Cemetery after March 1, 1898. A second ordinance further prohibited internments within city limits after August 1, 1901. By 1904, this eviction of the dead from San Francisco caused the establishment of ten cemeteries in the vicinity of today's Colma.

Many famous family names have found their final resting place in Colma. Among these well-known dead are Ralston, Hearst, Flood, Parrott, Spreckels, Crocker, Hopkins, Strauss, and the native American, Ishi.

Ishi was the last surviving California Native American, and lived much of his life as his ancestors had, in the mountains of northern California. In his last days, he worked with the scholars at the California Academy of Sciences and the University of California to record the language and history of his people. Ishi died on March 25, 1916, and his ashes were placed in a small black pueblo jar with the inscription, ''Ishi, The Last Yana Indian.''

As you enter Colma from Highway 280 along Hickey Boulevard, you are aware of the unyielding mass of San Bruno Mountain advancing into the valley from the north. Turn toward the mountain along El Camino Real and shortly the row of cemeteries appears along the bay side of the road. Many of the cemeteries welcome visitors for some moments of thoughtful remembrance.

You may want to stop at Malloy's Brooksville Hotel on Mission Road (Mission Road parallels El Camino Real). Here many a departed friend has been toasted for the last time. Malloy's always enjoys a raucous Halloween when the owners dust off an old casket and set it out for anyone brave enough to sit in it and have their picture taken. Although this city may seem all peace and tranquillity, Malloy's Tavern adds a jovial note for residents and visitors.

Crystal Springs Dam

In 1890, headlines trumpeted the achievement of the largest concrete dam in the world. The 1906 Earthquake caused an eight foot displacement next to the dam, but did no damage to the dam itself, and after this, Crystal Springs Dam was declared the safest dam in the United States.

All this excitement began in the 1860s with Hermann Schussler, a young German engineer, who guided the Spring Valley Water Company's watershed expansion. Under Schussler's direction the company corralled all of San Mateo's runoff for San Francisco. The centerpiece for this accomplishment is the Crystal Springs Dam on the east side of Lower Crystal Springs Reservoir.

In 1868 Schussler designed the San Andreas Dam and, ten years later, built the earthen Old Crystal Springs Dam that supports Highway 92 between Upper and Lower Crystal Springs Reservoirs. These conventional dams of the day were preludes to the genius of concrete dams. Built across the San Mateo Creek, the Crystal Springs Dam—the centerpiece of the water catchment system—became the engineering wonder of the late nineteenth century.

Hermann Schussler and William Bourn, the owner of the Spring Valley Water Company, kept their long range plans under wraps while Bourn quietly bought up the required parcels of land from local farmers. During this land acquisition, the celebrated Crystal Springs Hotel was also purchased by the water company as part of the overall plan.

For nearly fifty years the Crystal Springs Hotel had served the stage route to Half Moon Bay and Pescadero. In addition, wealthy San Franciscans

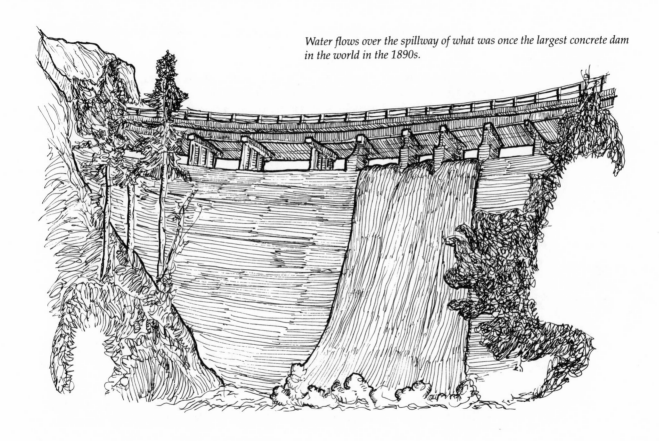

Water flows over the spillway of what was once the largest concrete dam in the world in the 1890s.

discovered this vacation hideaway where they could enjoy a lavish Sunday brunch of quail and champagne.

The first clue that local residents had of Bourn's plan was the sight of men clearing brush and the subsequent demolition of the Crystal Springs Hotel. Schussler's plan for a concrete dam called for large irregular but interlocking concrete blocks. Each block was individually poured and varied in size from six to ten feet in height, thirty to forty feet in length, and ten to fifteen feet wide.

After its completion, this giant concrete puzzle withstood the shock waves of the 1906 earthquake. The line of the San Andreas Fault lies within a few hundred feet of this 145 foot high dam. Nearby pipes that crossed the fault line were sheared in half and snapped out of the ground as the land shifted eight to nine feet to the north. The incredible flexibility of the interlocking blocks plus the strength of its design brought the dam through the quake without any damage.

In 1977, San Francisco Water and Power ordered a geologic and seismographic study of this structure. The survey company found that this historic dam meets all of today's earthquake safety standards.

Although visitors are not permitted on the dam itself, there is an overlook at the dam. Coming from San Francisco on Highway 280, take the Black Mountain Road exit. Then go south on Skyline Boulevard, which parallels the highway. The dam is located near Crystal Springs Road. From the overlook you can see the spillway and the mighty concrete creation.

Just before the overlook on Skyline Boulevard, Sawyer Camp Historic Trail is located on watershed property and open to the public. This historic trail begins some distance north of the dam near Crystal Springs Road and Skyline Boulevard.

Jepson Laurel Tree.

Although the trail is bordered on each side by a chain link fence to prevent intrusion onto watershed property, it remains one of the loveliest Peninsula walks no matter what time of the year. Along this trail walkers encounter the largest California Bay tree, the Jepson Laurel. There is a rest stop with picnic tables, where you can compare your guesses of the tree's size with those entered on the 1920 commemorative plaque.

At the time of the plaque's dedication, this venerable giant was declared the second largest bay tree in existence. However, since then, the previously largest tree has fallen. Thus, it can be said that the Jepson Laurel now stands as the largest bay tree in the world.

With these superlatives in both concrete and massive tree, a visit to the Crystal Springs Reservoirs is a day to remember.

Skyline Boulevard runs
between Sawyer Camp Trail
and the scenic dam turn-out.

47

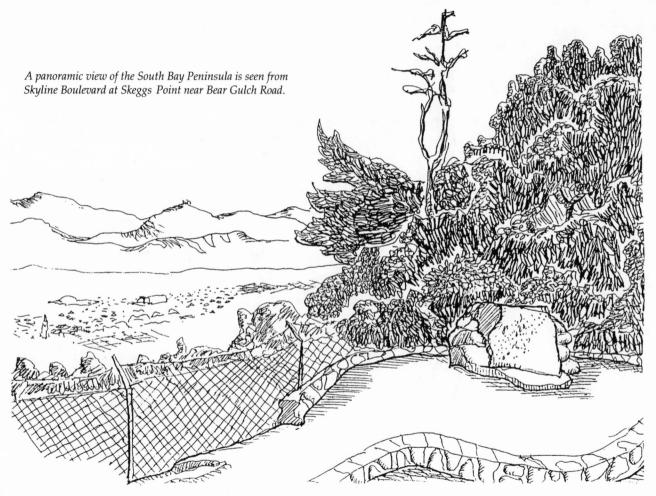

A panoramic view of the South Bay Peninsula is seen from
Skyline Boulevard at Skeggs Point near Bear Gulch Road.

48

King's Mountain

King's Mountain, part of the Santa Cruz Range, overlooks the Peninsula landscape as lesser hills rumple northward like a golden carpet in the summer sun. The mountain's moist climate and neutral soils stimulate forest growth. As a result, the mountain is covered with a second growth forest of redwoods, douglas fir and other conifers.

Along the creeks and hills a chaparral, that is made up of ever-green buckeye, sage, sumac, wild blackberry, mountain huckleberry, scrub oak, and poison oak, runs wild. Gray-green in color, this pervasive growth prevents erosion and holds ground moisture.

Once the home of grizzly bears and mountain lions, the mountain's animal population has been changed by encroaching cities. Mountain lions are occasionally spotted in the less populated recesses of the wild area, but the grizzlies are gone.

The area has a Mediterranean climate, with mild, wet winters and dry summers. The height of these mountains protects the bayside communities from the ocean fog that funnels through the 500-foot-wide Crystal Springs Gap and through the 300-foot-wide San Bruno Gap.

Looking north toward San Bruno Mountain, the action of plate tectonics becomes obvious. The Crystal Springs Reservoir rests in the valley formed by a millennia of action between the American and Pacific plates. The Midpeninsula Regional Open Space District has best described this action in their guide to the fault zone: "The earth's outer skin is a jigsaw puzzle of 60 mile thick plates floating on a sea of plastic rock. When two plates move against each other the rock breaks and forms an area of weakness called a fault zone."

The famous San Andreas fault runs along Crystal Springs Reservoir then north through Thornton Beach. Along this 600-mile fault, which extends from Mexico through Northern California, the Pacific plate is grinding northwestward past the American plate. Because of this movement, stones have been found on the west side of the fault zone that occur only on the slopes of mountains located far to the south. Numerous examples of such displacement demonstrate this inexorable movement northward of the westerly plate. The San Andreas fault derives its name from the small San Andres Creek that was dammed by the Spring Valley Water Company.

Here on King's Mountain, Huddart Park was formed in the 1940s as part of the development of riding and hiking trails. Along Skyline Boulevard two trails plunge into the redwood and fir forest. The parking is limited at these upper extremities of Huddart, but within a short distance from Skyline both the Richard's Road and the Summit Springs Trails offer a look into the area's now-vanished lumber industry.

For a look at the lower park area and the many activities offered there, take King's Mountain Road to the east until you reach the park entrance on your left. A fee scale includes day use or family camping rates. There is no fee for backpackers but advance reservations are necessary. The longer trails take you into the heart of the redwoods along cool creek beds. Huddart offers some of the finest hiking in San Mateo County.

A short distance south of Skeggs Point, a twisted redwood escaped the lumberman's saw in the last century. This Methuselah of the forest measures 55 feet in circumference. A small parking space on the east side of the road marks the path leading to this spared giant.

Filoli

Filoli stands as a man's dream, an architect's statement, and a gardener's heaven. Nestled in the Coast Range on watershed land, Filoli opens its gates to the wondering eyes of visitors from all parts of the world. Once the grand home of William Bowers Bourn II, the estate and grand manor house titillate the senses and stir the imagination of everyone that travels the oak-shaded entrance.

The turn of the century saw the powerful mastery of Bourn joined with the architectural genius of Willis J. Polk to create the masterpiece, Filoli. The name reflects the motto that ruled the driven nature of Bourn: Fight, Love, Live. To know their meaning is to understand the nature of the first master of Filoli.

After interrupting his studies at Cambridge University and upon his father's death, William B. Bourn II took possession of the family gold mine in Grass Valley, California, and developed the mine into a success. Then, in 1907, he turned his voracious eyes to the Spring Valley Water Company whose buildings, water pipes, and pumps were in shambles following the great 1906 earthquake. He purchased this sole supplier of water to San Francisco and began three decades of work to establish a comprehensive company. In 1930, after repairs, consolidation, and a massive construction program, he sold the Spring Valley Company to the people of San Francisco for $41 million.

While developing his company, Bourn also developed plans with Willis Polk for the construction of a mixed-style Georgian manor house. He employed

Filoli's main entrance has a massive sliding door that covers the front door when inclement weather buffets the courtyard.

Bruce Porter to design the formal gardens. In 1915, work began on Filoli and within two years the family occupied the house although work continued on the upper story.

Construction of various outbuildings was delayed by World War I and by this time Bourn and Polk had ceased speaking to each other. Bourn objected to Polk's fondness for alcohol and began placing his commission in a trust fund for Mrs. Polk. Consequently, the design of the carriage house and adjacent buildings were drawn by Arthur Brown, Jr.

When the Bourn's daughter, Maud, married in 1910, William Bourn purchased the Muckross Estate in Ireland as a home for the newlyweds. Some stories are told that Filoli's design is based on this Irish estate. Although Bourn frequently visited this Irish country home while a student at Cambridge, there exists little resemblance between the two. However, Bourn did commission Ernest Peixotto to execute Filoli's ballroom murals of the Muckross Estate overlooking the lakes of Killarney.

''Lake'' views, as Bourn called Crystal Springs reservoirs, once enhanced the north wing. Now the willows have grown too tall, and there is no longer a view of San Francisco's water supply.

Bourn oversaw the detail design of the estate grounds to preserve this essential ruggedness of nature. The gardens were purposely placed in the same axis as the house and lying to the south. In this way the vistas from the house proper promote a sense of tamed nature dissolving into the green canopy of the Coast Range. This effect is contrived most notably in the sunken garden, where the viewer's eyes are drawn ever higher into the hills. The Irish yews that surround this special glade were grown from Muckross Abbey seedlings.

The garden has been tended by the careful hands of women since the inception of the estate. Initially, Isabella Worn arranged for the flower selection to complete Bruce Porter's designs. Continuity with the original plans was

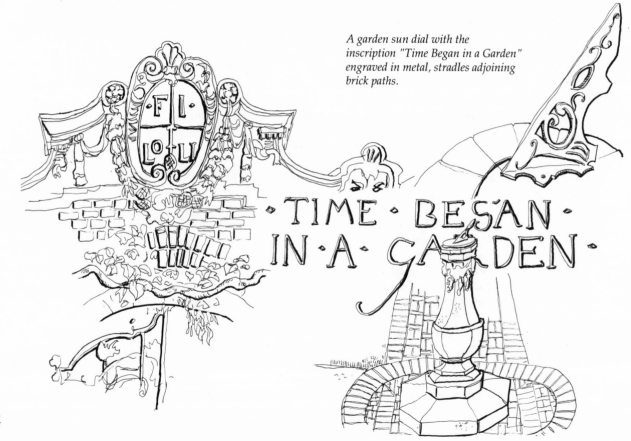

A brick wall with an ornamental iron arch separates one of the Filoli gardens.

A garden sun dial with the inscription "Time Began in a Garden" engraved in metal, stradles adjoining brick paths.

FI LO LI

TIME · BEGAN · IN · A · GARDEN ·

possible even after the deaths of Mr. and Mrs. Bourn in 1936. When the estate was purchased by Mr. and Mrs. William P. Roth in that same year, Isabella Worn continued as head gardener. After her departure in 1948, Mrs. Roth pursued her keen interest in the garden. The gardens, now mature, benefited from the harmonious additional plantings made during the nearly forty years of Mrs. Roth's occupancy. Today, the gardens continue in this tradition under the care of Lucy Tolmach, Garden Superintendent.

The gardens boast flower plantings that offer heady blooms whatever the season of the year. The quaint Knot Garden finds its inspiration in medieval European herb gardens. In the Chartres Cathedral Garden the boxwood borders represent the lead outlines of a stained glass window. Other gardens in the magnificent display are the Sunken Garden, the Walled Garden, the Woodland Garden, Yew Allee, and the Rose Garden. In the various seasons azaleas, camellias, magnolias, rhododendrons, and roses provide splashes of brilliant color.

In 1975, Mrs. Roth gave the generous parcel of land which includes the house and gardens, to the National Trust for Historic Preservation. The house and gardens are open for tours from mid-February until mid-November on Tuesdays through Saturdays. Advance reservations are necessary and there is an admission charge. For reservations and information contact Friends of Filoli at (415) 364-2880.

Filoli transports the visitor to an era of ''gracious living.'' With a masterful combination of light, color and human endeavor, Filoli invites late twentieth century man to linger and absorb its peace and tranquillity.

Woodside Store

In 1849, the Gold Rush called men from all parts of the country to find their fortune in California's Mother Lode. In that year, Matthias Alfred Parkhurst, a young man of 20, arrived in San Mateo County and put down roots by purchasing land.

He applied the name "Woodside" to his 127 acre parcel of timberland. Later, he used this name for his store and the post office. At the beginning of the American period, there were in these hills a dozen or more sawmills and shingle mills in operation. The mountain slopes were covered with trails leading into the heart of the virgin redwood forest.

Early on, there was a well defined trail from present day Redwood City to Parkhurst's land. After 1850 this trail became known as Searsville Road and today it is called Woodside Road. Other active roads in this period had forks that led to Parkhurst's "Woodside."

In 1868 the toll road known as the San Gregorio–Redwood City Turnpike, which is today's King's Mountain Road, took travelers to the summit of the Coast Range. Although this turnpike was established five years after Parkhurst's death, his store determined the beginning of this toll road. Travelers along this turnpike stopped at the Woodside Store before attacking the steep grade.

The beginnings of the Woodside Store rest in the hands of four men: Parkhurst, Robert O. Tripp, Grizzly Ryder and a man known only as Ellis. Tripp and Ryder served together in the Mexican War and, at the end of that war, traveled to California. They made no effort to reach the gold fields, but

M. Alfred Parkhurst and Robert O.
Tripp's early pioneer country store
during the lumberjack and
gold-mining days of California.

57

decided instead to leave the city life of San Francisco and engage in the lumbering business.

Tripp and Ryder established camp near Parkhurst's "Woodside" and began cutting out piles for the San Francisco wharves under construction during that city's boom. They hauled the lumber to present day Redwood City, which was then called "Embarcadero," and employed the bay waters and tides to float their timbers to San Francisco—a common method of delivery. The partnership ended after Ryder was severely mauled by a grizzly bear and returned to Massachusetts with his wife. It is believed that, around 1850, Ellis went to the gold fields after Parkhurst bought Ellis' share of the business.

With Ellis and Ryder out of the picture, Parkhurst invited Tripp to become his partner. They consolidated their enterprises and formed Tripp & Parkhurst. Sometime in 1851, they began a mercantile business alongside the lumbering operations. In the fall of that year, they opened a store in a cabin on the site of the present Tripp house, just southeast of the Woodside Store. Parkhurst maintained the books for this venture and in these ledgers after July 21, 1853, he designated the store's location as "Woodside."

Parkhurst was responsible for the establishment of a post office at the store which was the terminus for a regular stage service between "Woodside" and San Francisco. He assigned the name Woodside to the post office and provided the necessary office space in a new two-story store which he built across the road from the original cabin-store.

The Woodside store also served as one of several places in the county where the Tax Collector spent a day each fall to collect State and County taxes. Tradition holds that Tripp also used the store to provide privacy for people while he extracted their teeth. Dentistry in the timbering country was rudimentary with only a shot of whiskey to kill the pain.

An 1859 advertisement, shows the store had a wide variety of goods available, including clothing, dry goods, farm equipment, hardware, groceries, and provisions. The business thrived while serving the needs of the local community.

In 1860 rumors began to fly that the Tripp and Parkhurst partnership was about to be dissolved. However, they reached an agreement in which Parkhurst controlled the store activities while Tripp supervised the ranch operations.

In 1863, after a long illness, Parkhurst died at his beloved "Woodside." Recent research by historian Dorothy Regnery revealed that Parkhurst died without a will although he held considerable property. In this vacuum, Tripp petitioned the County Court for appointment as a Special Administrator of the estate. This appointment gave him the power to take over the store and conduct an inventory of the stock.

As estate administrator, Tripp evaluated the properties with gross misrepresentations and undervaluations. Parkhurst had died without descendants or spouse, so that his father and step-mother were the sole heirs. The elder Parkhursts lived in Massachusetts, but were alerted to Tripp's miscalculations on the extensive value of the estate.

In 1867, after some legal wrangling, Tripp agreed to pay Matthias Parkhurst an additional $1,000 for his son's share of the Woodside acreage. Even with this additional money, Regnery's research has revealed that the total amount paid was still much below the property's value.

Tripp lived on in Woodside until his death in 1906. He was the sole survivor of the four men who established the Woodside Store.

As concluded by Dorothy F. Regnery in the June 1987 issue of *La Peninsula*, the journal of the San Mateo County Historical Association: "The '49er Parkhurst should be given the credit due him for the purchase and naming of the 127 acres "Woodside," the origin of the present community. He was the person responsible for the creation of a store on the property, for obtaining one of the earliest post offices in San Mateo County, to which was applied the name Woodside, and for the operation of the remote, rural store until his death. Because Parkhurst died young, with no heirs, his significant pioneer role was soon forgotten. Hopefully in the future Parkhurst's founding role will be recognized.''

The Woodside Store Museum tells the story of this historic building that served as post office, general store, dentist's office and library. A hands-on experience awaits the visitor with the trade items of the 1850s overflowing every bin. The scales are operational along with the apple press, bean sorter and blacksmith's tools.

There is no admission charge for the Woodside Store Museum, located at the corner of Tripp and Woodside Roads. Call (415) 851-7615 for the schedule of open days and hours, which vary with the seasons.

Like Parkhurst, today's visitor notices the warm sunshine and gentle breezes of this valley. The redwood timber that brought the sawyers in the 1850s is gone, but a special community of gentlemen farmers, gentlemen ranchers, exurbanites and horses has taken their place.

Pioneer Hotel

WOODSIDE

Rustic Woodside, with notices of equestrian events, boarding horses and trading same for a better deal, hardly reflects the early days of whiskey stills in the ravines and tough brawls in the bars. But, as the lumbering ventures dried up, new homes were built on graceful estates and Woodside Village developed at the junction of roads leading north, south, east and west. Simple general stores, butcher shop, blacksmith and post office developed to serve the summer estates and landed gentry.

The birth of the Pioneer Hotel around 1878 rests in the clouded history of Whiskey Hill. In that year John Hadler completed his residence and built a saloon as a regular stop for the stage coaches headed toward Pescadero and Spanish Town.

In 1884 Captain Peter Hanson bought the saloon and adjacent buildings. Promptly he changed the name to Hanson's Exchange. He removed most of the out buildings and all of the original saloon except the front of the present Pioneer Hotel.

In 1914 Peter Mathieson bought the land and buildings from the Hanson family. The Mathieson family operated the hotel, restaurant, and saloon until the close of World War II. As the era of the automobile dawned with long drives into the countryside, business improved for the Pioneer Hotel. The new owners, Aldo and Bodee Comonoli modernized the interior and changed the dark western bar into a cocktail lounge with live dance music.

At the crest of the hill this relic of an old West hotel greets the traveller's eye.

When Aldo Comonoli died his widow, Bodee, found that operating the hotel and restaurant alone proved to be difficult. So, in 1963 she sold a portion of the hotel to the Wells Fargo Bank for their offices. And, by 1966 the restaurant was no longer in operation.

The present owners, Leonard and Dorothee Dary, with son Brad, have continued this long tradition of an old country tavern. The intimate atmosphere comes complete with redwood burl tables, stained glass, and on chilly nights a blazing fireplace. There is dancing to live music six nights a week (except Mondays). Several bands appear regularly and the congenial crowd enjoys this country western sound.

Another long survivor in the area was Neuman's General Store which was built by Andre Neuman, Oakland nurseryman, who was also responsible for the first eucalyptus trees in the area.

Even winemaking was attempted in the area at the turn of the century by Agoston Haraszthy, who was one of the founders of commercial viticulture in California. After some unsuccessful attempts in the damp environment of the Crystal Springs Valley, now inundated by the reservoir, he left for Sonoma County where his name continues in the winemaking industry.

Woodside's sunny climate and mild winters attracted San Francisco tycoons during the Gilded Age. These new landed squires sought isolation in the same wooded canyons that had sheltered fugitives from the law.

As cities encroached from the east these citizens formed a city that was never intended to become one in a real sense. Large homesteads are the rule and the adage ''no sidewalks'' remains the standard to project a country image.

Woodside charms the visitor and lulls the senses to a slower pace. Even a brief visit to these crossroads leaves the traveler with a sense of an elegant past filled with mansions and well maintained stables.

Folger Stables in Wunderlich Park may evoke memories of old
Kentucky and its living quarters for race horses.

Wunderlich Park

The combination of Edwardian splendor and the ruggedness of mountain forests makes Wunderlich Park a hiker's paradise. Located just two miles southwest of Woodside on the Woodside Road, this undeveloped park offers 25 miles of hiking and equestrian trails.

The focal point in the park is the Folger Stables, designed in 1905 by Arthur Brown, Jr., for the "Coffee King" James A. Folger. The stables carry out the architectural theme developed for the estate. The deep dormers and ground floor arcades resemble the main house's porches.

These were the days of carriages and fine horses and the stables to match their importance. The interior cobblestones contrast with the pink marble baseboards and mahogany paneling. In the tack room, a marble fireplace completes the picture of luxury.

Folger dammed a creek on the property and used the waterfall to turn a turbine. Thus, he developed the state's first hydroelectric plant in 1904. When electricity reached Woodside, the dam and plant were dismantled.

The property passed from the Folger family to Martin Wunderlich in 1956. In a generous donation, Wunderlich gave 924 acres of the estate to San Mateo County for the park. The County developed an extensive trail system by using old logging roads and constructing new loops to connect a network of fine trails.

The Meadow Trail leads hikers to high meadows, which offer excellent vistas in all seasons and scores of wild flowers in the springtime. Other trails lead into the second growth redwood forest with massive stumps left from the logging of the 1850s. This virgin forest contained trees eight feet or more in diameter and thousands of years old. Along the steep, moist canyons, sword ferns with their Christmas stocking-shaped leaves grow from the walls and the giant chain fern brushes the trail.

These well-marked trails challenge the best available in the county. The blending of a mixed forest with open meadows brings the best habitat for birds. Veteran bird watchers discover a wide mix of birds throughout the park. Even the novice can sight a bright blue jay darting from the oaks to the brush. Hawks circle above the meadows and deer are frequently seen along the trails or in the meadows.

Wunderlich Park is a haven of solitude and an opportunity to join nature in a setting near the developing suburbs. In any season this network of trails beckons the city dweller to pack a lunch and head for a new adventure in the park.

La Honda

As a brilliant rocket lighting up the sky, La Honda burst on the world scene in the 1960s with Ken Kesey's Pranksters who from their simple cabin rocked the country with the wildness of their trips aboard a crazy quilt bus. While at home, Kesey and company turned the town topsy turvy with wild parties and police raids.

Today, these are simply memories that linger with the small talk in the local restaurants and bars. For most travelers La Honda is a brief stop on the scenic roads to San Gregorio, Pescadero or Sam McDonald Park.

Sam McDonald Park is a rugged park with changes in terrain from 400 feet at Alpine Creek to 1300 feet at Towne Ridge. On each of these levels, vegetation varies from the redwood forest along the steep ravines to grasslands at the higher elevations. Headquarters for the park are located at 13435 Pescadero Road, on the edge of the 870-acre preserve. With trails connecting to Pescadero Creek Park, San Mateo County Memorial Park, and Portola State Park, this area offers the long distance hiker numerous options.

Camping in the park is open only to youth groups in accord with the wishes of Sam McDonald. At park headquarters a photo display tells the story of Sam McDonald, who was the son of slaves and for 50 years worked as a grounds keeper and later as a grounds superintendent for Stanford University beginning in 1903. During World War I Sam McDonald began acquiring land, starting with the La Honda property with a two room cabin along Alpine

Creek. At his death in 1957 he had acquired 400 acres which he left to Stanford University to be used as a park for young people. In the 1970s, adjacent land was purchased by the county to bring the park to its present size.

Adults may stay overnight in the park at a Sierra Club Hiking Hut located a mile and half from headquarters. Reservations with a modest fee are necessary for this Danish styled hut and can be made by calling (415) 327-8111. The hikers' hut holds up to 14 people and is fully equipped. The hikers need to bring only personal items, a sleeping bag and food.

A short distance from this park, Heritage Grove offers a special opportunity to walk among the redwoods. This small park is located on Alpine Road one mile east of Pescadero Road. Heritage Grove covers just 37 acres and was saved in the 1970s by the quick action of a group of alert citizens. The redwoods in this park had been spared in the last century, and one day someone noticed that the trees were marked with blue paint—a telltale sign of the coming chain saws. A community effort ensued to prevent the cutting of these giants and raised half the money needed to save the grove.

The chain saws are gone and the sawmills silenced. The redwood groves around La Honda hold the story of nature's persistence in the face of insurmountable odds. Each visitor to these woods can savor this spirit of regeneration and capture the vitality of growth.

LA HONDA

A one room schoolhouse from the lumberjack days still exists as a private residence.

69

Typical water tower and storage room on Jellich Apple Ranch, Portola Road, Portola Valley

Alpine Inn

Pick up the gauntlet of youth and drop daily cares for a few hours. Return to the familiar haunt of students, The Alpine Inn, in the hills behind Stanford University. Located at 3915 Alpine Road, this rustic building has been a roadhouse since the 1850s.

The roadhouse was started over a hundred years ago by Felix Buelna, an early Californio. The son of a poet, he was not equipped for the life of a rancher and decided to establish a roadhouse on land given him by his daughter's father-in-law. Buelna served as *Alcalde* of Pueblo de San Jose and was well liked by his fellow Spanish-speaking people. In addition to watering their horses, he quenched his patrons' thirst with whiskey. On Sundays the old establishment came alive with fellow Californios seeking entertainment. The American city fathers in San Jose passed ordinances outlawing Sabbath-breaking activities, such as, gambling and bull-or-bear baiting.

Felix prospered until one day he fell prey to his own entertainments and lost the roadhouse in a poker game. Then a wild assortment of owners and proprietors descended upon the Alpine Inn and with each one a new name was painted on the false front. The many owners reflect the kaleidoscope of nationalities in the county—Italian, Irish, German, and Portuguese.

The existence of the Alpine Inn has always been tenuous. However, in recent years some respectability arrived at the doorstep with its designation as a registered State Historic Landmark and its placement on the National Register.

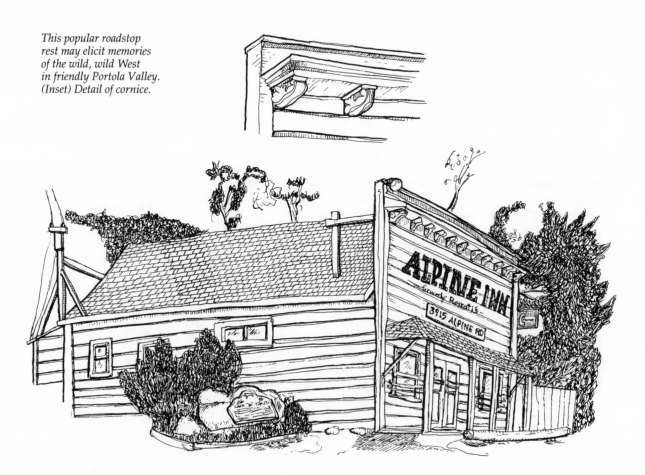

This popular roadstop
rest may elicit memories
of the wild, wild West
in friendly Portola Valley.
(Inset) Detail of cornice.

A stone castle gatehouse of Willow Brook Farm on Portola Road, built by Herbert Law, who helped finance the rebuilding of San Francisco's Fairmont Hotel after the 1906 earthquake.

The Alpine Inn retains a special aura despite its new status. Infinite numbers of patrons have left their carved mark on the wooden tabletops. This carving transcends graffiti to become folk art at its best.

The wide cross section of people stopping at the Alpine Inn reflects the continuing population diversity of the Peninsula. An air of comradeship fills the rooms at anytime of year. On warm sunny days people carry their food and drinks outdoors to the picnic tables under the live oaks and bay trees.

A nearby creek bed gurgles after the rainy season. With these sounds the stolen moments of youth return to flood the memory of those who take the time to linger at the Alpine Inn.

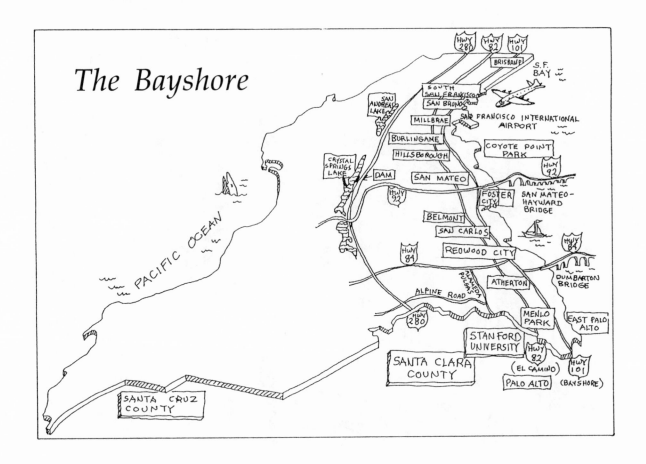

The Bayshore

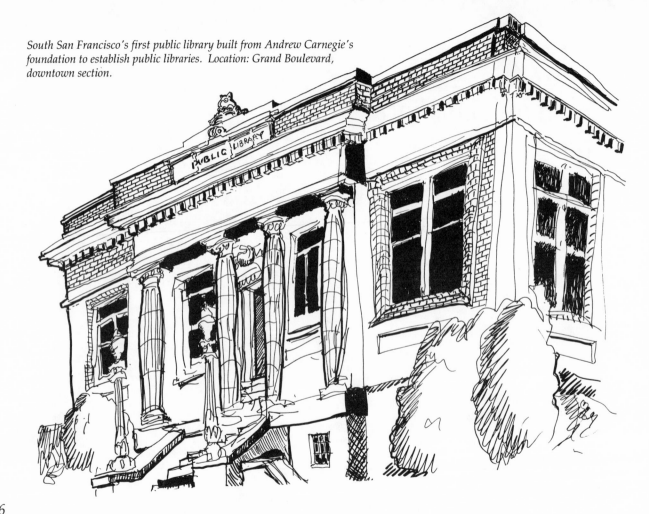

South San Francisco's first public library built from Andrew Carnegie's foundation to establish public libraries. Location: Grand Boulevard, downtown section.

South San Francisco

Known the world over as "The Industrial City," South San Francisco has proclaimed its existence from Sign Hill since 1923. In that year the Chamber of Commerce promoted business with slogans such as: "Think well of your town, speak well of it, remember you live here, buy here," and, "Keep your tax dollars at home." These ambitious statements rival today's television advertising campaigns. The city fathers knew well the advantages of a good ad campaign. Here with the words, "The Industrial City," spelled in painted concrete, the city has attained international name recognition with thousands of world travelers who pass the flanks of Sign Hill as they head north from San Francisco International Airport.

Entrepreneurship formed the basis for South San Francisco even at the outset. In 1888, Gustavus Swift scouted the area for a suitable location for his meat packing and stock yard operation to supply the growing population of Northern California. South San Francisco presented a suitable location because it had a natural harbor on the bay for transportation, it had prevailing winds from the ocean which would carry the obnoxious odors away from proposed residential areas, and there was the prospect for railroad transportation as well. Swift approached other meat packing giants in the midwest and the South San Francisco Land and Improvement Company was formed.

By 1908 the city incorporated and annexed the small dairy community of Baden. South San Francisco began the journey to become The Industrial City. Although meat packing remained a major industry, other enterprises flocked to the city.

South San Francisco also had its truck farms in the foothills.

Pottery and brick manufacturing relied on the natural supply of clay from the adjacent hills. Lumber mills received the giant redwoods from the coast range. Rice packers depended on the marsh lands of the bay. Later, shipyards and steel mills joined these early industries.

With the luster of success comes the tarnish of crime. South San Francisco was no exception. During Prohibition the city with its established wharves and numerous ''soft drink'' establishments, became the center for bootlegging operations. The daily press provided the citizenry with frequent stories of smuggler arrests and the closing of another speakeasy.

The hard working citizens enjoyed the simple pleasures of socializing with each other in baseball clubs, fraternal organizations, and church groups. As early as 1911 the women of the Violet Club gathered for their first meeting and had their picture taken. The young men of the community formed their own group with the winsome title of the Disappointed Bachelors. No record exists to say if they ever held a joint meeting.

As the city grew in population and importance, the need for a new civic center became a pressing concern. A committee of prominent citizens scoured the state for a suitable model but found none to meet their dream for South San Francisco. At last architects were petitioned to submit plans. Architects Werner and Coffey developed plans that called for a replica of Independence Hall in Philadelphia. At last South San Francisco found a city hall to fill their dreams.

Today, this city hall continues to rise as a special feature of the landscape as it overlooks the surrounding neat pattern of streets. ''South City'' is rapidly becoming a center for the growing bio-technology industry.

*Grand Boulevard
street lamp.*

Brisbane

From a distance the houses of Brisbane appear to cling to the hillside like Swiss chalets awaiting the winter snows. But, snow never reaches these tidy homes that add Christmas cheer to all who pass with a lighted star atop each house.

Another Brisbane tradition since the bicentennial celebration are the colorful fire hydrants. These patriotic symbols brighten the city's streets and bring compliments from visitors.

Brisbane counts its earliest beginnings with the 1906 earthquake. At that time, promoters laid out streets, installed sidewalks, and waited for the residents to appear. However, two decades later editor Arthur Brisbane visited the area and found the valley vacant. As the story is told, Brisbane predicted that this lovely valley, so favored by nature, could not long remain vacant.

If the story is true,, some say the city was named after him when the community decided to incorporate in 1961. Others say that the name was selected because of similarities to the Australian city.

No matter which story is true, Brisbane retains the flavor of an Alpine village as it presses against San Bruno Mountain. To experience the fine views of the bay and lower peninsula, go north along Bayshore Boulevard to Guadalupe Canyon Parkway and turn west. At the junction with Radio Road turn left and proceed to the crest of San Bruno Mountain.

This mountain is the last refuge of ecosystems that flourished for thousands of years around the Bay Area. Six rare and endangered species of plants share these mountain slopes. Although San Mateo County has designated San Bruno Mountain as a suitable regional park, the final stages of the plan remain unresolved.

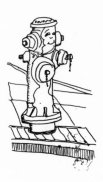

Brisbane decorates its water hydrants.

Alpine villa houses on Brisbane's hillside with Christmas star decorations.

This Roman Renaissance Revival water main tower was built under the Spring Valley Water Company. Location: Near San Andreas Water Filter Plant, San Bruno.

San Bruno

Immediately after the 1906 earthquake and fire, refugees of San Francisco's inferno fled south along county roads with fear tugging at their coats. San Bruno stood in the path of these fleeing families. Enterprising real estate agents strung banners over the main roads offering ''free camping'' and ''free provisions.'' Many simply diverted traffic to their sales offices where a homesite could be acquired for only $5 down and $5 a month.

With the tragedy of San Francisco came the birth of San Bruno. Overnight the city was born. By 1914 the populace was tired of plank sidewalks over mud-ridden streets and poor public service. In one day the Volunteer Fire Department staged a carnival and collected the necessary signatures to hold an election for incorporation as a city.

The early city catered to the suburban commuter and ranks as one of the Peninsula's first bedroom communities. The location of the city at the crossroads of El Camino Real and San Bruno Toll Road, now San Mateo Avenue, primed the area for recreational outlets as well.

At this junction two establishments provided the easy outlet for fun and frolic. For almost 75 years the Junction House and Uncle Tom's Cabin combined to offer food, lodging and entertainment. In the early days, lodging was simple and the meals straightforward. But, under the ownership of August Jenevein, Uncle Tom's Cabin offered excellent French dining with fine wines. The property became a social gathering place with a baseball park and, under the eucalyptus and cypress trees, a picnic grove with a raised platform for dancing.

*Jenevein's House at
905 Jenevein Avenue, San Bruno.*

Located near the railroad and trolley lines, the Tanforan Racetrack enjoyed continuing crowds even through the era of wagerless horse racing. When not in use as a horse track, Tanforan held early car races and air shows.

During the two world wars, this large open area with easy access to roads and rail transportation attracted the attention of the military. Under the 1942 Executive Order calling for the internment of all Japanese on the West Coast, Tanforan Racetrack was used as a temporary holding area while more permanent sites were prepared. Between May and September of that year, the racetrack saw the passing of over 4000 Japanese Americans on their way to internment camps.

After the war, racing resumed and continued until 1963 when the race season was cancelled and activities moved to Bay Meadows in San Mateo. Today, the Tanforan Shopping Center covers a major portion of the old racetrack.

For most of its existence, San Bruno has served the needs of commuters and travelers. With the development of the San Francisco International Airport along its border, San Bruno became a link to a world of travelers.

Spring Valley Water Company

Spring Valley Water Company has ridden the crest of the wave in supplying water to San Francisco. "More water," has been the cry from the great city to the north. Like a thirsty tiger, the city's and peninsula's needs seem boundless.

The Spring Valley Water Company was formed in 1860 during the booming growth of San Francisco when the small water company within the city was failing to meet demands. The company laid some lines from a spring located near Washington and Mason Streets in San Francisco. From these meager beginnings came a monolithic empire.

On July 4, 1862, the real colors of this company began to shine with the completion of a 32-mile redwood flume, which ran from Pilarcitos Creek in San Mateo County. San Franciscans went wild on that Fourth of July, having water in abundance to supply their present and future needs. The triumph of technology dazzled their imaginations and the San Francisco Water Works saw the handwriting on the wall. In three short years they were gobbled up and the Spring Valley Water Company moved forward.

In 1867, more water was made available with the creation of Pilarcitos Dam and Lake. Today this reservoir continues to supply water to the City of San Francisco and stands as the oldest dam on the Peninsula. Pilarcitos Lake is surrounded by watershed property and a California State Fish and Game Preserve. With this dual designation, the lake and dam are not open to the public and remain as a wilderness preserve in the midst of a metropolitan area.

An elaborate water meter cover and a corrugated sheetmetal pumphouse
remain in Millbrae at the former Spring Valley Water Company yard.

In the last half of the nineteenth century, the San Andreas and the two Crystal Spring Dams were completed. Then, the nightmare of the 1906 earthquake and fire struck. Buildings, pipe lines, mains, and pump stations lay in ruin. The company wavered and in the panic of 1907 banks refused to finance needed reconstruction. With matters in severe recession, William B. Bourn II stepped into the picture and bought the failing company.

Quickly this keen master of entrepreneurship took the necessary steps to insure financial solvency. Bourn continued to harness the forces of nature for San Francisco. Willis Polk, the well-known architect, helped in the design of headquarter's buildings at 1000 El Camino Real in Millbrae. Some of the smaller buildings remain on this property today.

Bourn turned his attention to providing more water for San Francisco with the purchase of land in Alameda County and the subsequent building of a major dam. When the City of San Francisco completed the O'Shaughnessy Dam and created the Hetch Hetchy Reservoir, this water source was leased to Spring Valley Water Company.

Bourn's business acumen seemed to touch everything. Political effort tried to unseat the Spring Valley Water Company's hold on the water supply of the city. In four election attempts between 1910 and 1927, bond issues failed to win the needed two-thirds majority to purchase the water company.

Finally, in May 1928, a $41 million bond issue to buy the Spring Valley Water Company passed. In 1930, ownership of all buildings, pumps, reservoirs, aqueducts, and riparian rights passed to San Francisco. Bourn felt this to be the height of his business accomplishments.

On October 24, 1934, the raging waters from Hetch Hetchy Reservoir joined the still waters of the Crystal Springs Lakes. This event was broadcast by radio to the residents of San Francisco and the Peninsula. The marvel of radio included the surge of waters as they mingled in the Pulgas Temple which was specially designed and constructed for the event. Today, a restored Temple area provides a favorite spot for sunbathing or a picnic. To reach the Pulgas Water Temple take Highway 280 to Edgewood Road, travel west along Edgewood until you reach Cañada Road and turn right and continue north on Canada. The temple is located on Cañada Road about a half mile north of the entrance to Filoli.

The Classical Greek structure has a central opening for viewing the waters as they rush through the Hetch Hetchy Aqueduct from Yosemite National Park. The landscaped grounds around the Pulgas Water Temple invite the visitor to linger and enjoy the tranquility of the lake region and reflect on the history of the Spring Valley Water Company.

For sixty years this company consistently supplied San Francisco with water and also amassed a vast holding of land on the Peninsula. As stipulated in the transfer to the City of San Francisco, this land is to be held, in perpetuity, as an ecological preserve that is devoted solely to water supply use. Because of Bourn's dedicated accomplishment, San Mateo's watershed lands provide an island of wilderness in a growing metropolitan area.

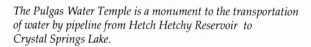

The Pulgas Water Temple is a monument to the transportation of water by pipeline from Hetch Hetchy Reservoir to Crystal Springs Lake.

Millbrae

*Former Spring Valley Water Company Supervisor's house,
now the Millbrae Historical Society Museum at the Civic Center.*

In 1866 Darius Ogden Mills built his three-story mansard roofed mansion on lands that he named "Millbrae" and so the roots of today's city were formed. By all standards this mansion was grand. The interior held a ballroom, art galleries, and two master bedrooms, one of ebony and the other of mother-of-pearl.

Millbrae was a proper setting for one of the "bonanza kings" who established his fortune during the Gold Rush and, eventually, joined William C. Ralston and the Bank of California. His fortune continued to grow as he acquired vast holdings in the Comstock mines.

Across El Camino from the estate, the Mills family pastured cows and this dairy venture continued long after the mansion had been designated for demolition. Today, the only reminders of the estate are the towering eucalyptus along El Camino Real. These scruffy trees were grown by Mills from Australian seeds.

Although much of the city's external history was lost with the demolition of the Darius O. Mills estate, the Millbrae Historical Society has collected and restored other memorabilia from the city's past.

To house these collections and to develop exhibits for the public, the society uses a former Spring Valley Water Company structure. Recently this supervisor's cottage was moved to One Constitution Square within the civic center complex.

To reach this former cottage and museum take the Millbrae Avenue exit from Highway 101 and travel west to Magnolia Avenue and turn right. At Library Avenue turn left. The area on your left is Constitution Square and Millbrae Civic Center.

Burlingame Railroad Depot

When you arrive at the Burlingame Railroad Station, turn your back to the building and look up Burlingame Avenue. Close your eyes for a moment and let the scene dissolve along with the noise of the modern city. Feel the warmth of Indian summer and hear the sounds of the open ranch land. Now, you have captured the scene as it appeared in October, 1894, when the Burlingame Depot opened.

Then the avenue was a simple dirt lane flanked by raw wooden fences. The depot stood as a spacious, solid base, linking the Burlingame Country Club at the top of the road with the outside world.

Two years prior, in 1892, the country club was formed by the heirs of San Francisco pioneer millionaires. For them the inconvenience of arriving at the flag stop station, Oak Grove, had become an intolerable nuisance.

With the club members' plight in mind, George H. Howard and others came to the rescue in 1893 by drawing up plans for a depot based on a new style introduced at the World's Fair in Chicago. Howard donated half the necessary land and the Burlingame Club members furnished the funds for the proposed $8,000 station. Negotiations were completed with Southern Pacific and work began on the new depot in 1893.

The style developed by Howard and J. B. Mathison for the railroad station became known as Mission Revival. Research shows that they incorporated elements from Stanford University, the California World's Fair and Exposition of 1893, and the early California missions.

From Stanford came the square tower and hipped roof. The missions contributed the curvilinear gables and the open arcade, complete with rounded arches supported by piers. From the Carmel Mission, Howard borrowed the concept of a Star Window over the platform.

The roof tiles used in the construction add considerably to the presentation of this Mission Revival style. The rich velvety texture of the tiles reveal their origins from the roofs of early California missions. The story of how these tiles manufactured by California Indians, reached the Burlingame Depot is shrouded in mystery. But, clearly the facts are that these large roof tiles were part of the Mission Dolores Asistencia in San Mateo and the San Antonio Mission in Jolon, Monterey County.

There is no doubt that these are eighteenth century Indian-made tiles. Their massive bulk contrasts significantly with the light airy quality of their shape.

The insulating effect of these tiles is felt in the interior of the depot on hot summer afternoons. The cool passenger waiting room with its large terra cotta floor recalls the ranchos that once covered the county.

The waiting room benches are the original dark bentwood seats. Their look of punched-out leather work invites memories of early California. Rail notices are still posted by the stationmaster on the dark oak bulletin board above the heater.

The first stationmaster, George Gates, arrived from Monterey as a newly married man just three days after his wedding. This caused some punsters to note that the depot has served even as a honeymoon cottage.

These early stationmasters found that living at the hub of a small community carried certain advantages. Mr. and Mrs. Gates recalled how everybody on the hill brought them items from their San Francisco shopping trips.

Today, the stationmaster's quarters are used as office space and the stationmaster keeps regular work hours that correspond to the train schedule. But, the depot counter, next to the large fan shaped window, is the original design.

A view of early Spanish Mission Revival train station formed by a private club in Hillsborough.

BVRLINGAME

A nearby location for a picnic, bike ride or bay swim is the Coyote Point Park. Take the Peninsula Avenue exit off Highway 101 and follow the signs for Coyote Point. The park also contains a breathtaking, environmental science museum designed by Palo Alto architect John W. Stypula. The museum stands in a grove of eucalyptus planted long ago by John McLaren. Every effort has been made to retain the flavor of this long time favorite among Bay Area parks. For information on the museum call (415) 573-2595.

Burlingame Country Club

The Burlingame Country Club is located in Hillsborough, not in Burlingame. When the club was first formed in the late nineteenth century by a group of wealthy San Franciscans, they created Burlingame along with an appropriate railroad station. These founders laid out a plan for their own rustic mansions and enjoyed this secluded arrangement.

After the 1906 earthquake and fire, droves of San Franciscans drifted south and discovered the blend of rustic charm with rail convenience. Within a short time the Country Club folk discovered a small city encroaching on their beloved terrain. They put their minds to the task and devised the perfect solution— form their own "city."

This scheme led to the formation of Hillsborough, a most unique community. Under State law at that time, each newly formed town had to provide a business district in their overall plan. The planners cleverly set aside an abandoned sand quarry as the business sector for their special town. In Hillsborough fashion, a rummage sale raised the first money for the required school. In other areas the legislature allowed newly formed towns more freedom. They established minimum lot sizes and building restrictions to discourage people of ordinary means. They planned a town without sidewalks, street lighting or curbs. Some public services were considered necessary, such as police and fire protection.

The heart of this deftly created community is the Burlingame Country Club. Fashioned after Maryland's Chevy Chase Club, it has remained a citadel of

A symbiotic relationship exists between the rich and poor,
landowner and servant, in this country club atmosphere.

96

Peninsula and San Francisco society. This country club was started in one of architect Arthur Page Brown's "cottages" between Floribunda and Bellevue Avenues on the old highway. A year later Brown executed some changes to one of the cottages and the club moved to this new location near present day Geri Lane and Forest View Road. After this move the club relocated two more times before settling in the present location which is the former William H. Crocker mansion, "New Place." The main gates are at New Place Road and Eucalyptus Avenue. Golf and tennis became the most popular club activities. However, the ultimate goal was to provide a full round of activities for these city folk in their rural retreat.

A polo field was developed on Howard property which today is bounded by Peninsula Avenue, Park Road, Howard Avenue and Highland Avenue. Horses were brought from old Spanish Town, today's Half Moon Bay, where surefooted and quick animals were a breeding tradition.

On May 12, 1903, President Theodore Roosevelt arrived at the Burlingame station and with a lavish parade he made his way up Burlingame Avenue to the club house. Although his speech was only a few sentences long, this day was long remembered by the members.

Memories live long in Hillsborough where families retain their homes in something akin to rustic splendor. This select community has retained the village air planned in 1893 and looks forward to the next century with confident serenity.

The Uplands

HILLSBOROUGH

A descending staircase marks the hallway near the front entrance with towering ceilings.

After Hillsborough incorporated, the town became a refuge for the wealthy of San Francisco. A flurry of estate planning began with architects finding employment. Two of these estates remain today in Hillsborough as a reminder of the celebration following the rebuilding of San Francisco after the earthquake and fire.

The dominant style of the 1915 Panama-Pacific International Exposition was Beaux-Arts Classical as demonstrated in Bernard Maybeck's Palace of Fine Arts. Today, San Francisco continues to enjoy this airy creation in its Marina district. The melancholy scene, with columns and porticos reflected in the pond, preserves the Maybeck style for the public.

The two homes built in Hillsborough during this celebration era were Uplands and Carolands. Both of these mansions remain today as architectural examples of this period.

Willis Polk designed Uplands for Charles Templeton Crocker, the son of Charles F. Crocker. The elder Crocker had lived at this site in a dark brown Swiss Chalet until his death in 1897. The Swiss Chalet never satisfied C. Templeton Crocker who determined a grand villa would be more appropriate.

The first order of business was the removal of the unwanted Swiss Chalet. Charles Templeton Crocker offered the four story, thirty-six room house to a local contractor, Charles T. Lindgren, on the condition that Lindgren remove the house from the property without damaging any trees. Lindgren owned property adjacent to Crocker but across San Mateo Creek.

The Grand manner of French architecture can be seen at Uplands with its balustraded parapets, twin columns and deceptively simple double-hung windows.

In the June 1916 issue of *Popular Mechanics*, Lindgren described the precarious journey of the house down the glen and across the creek bed. Horses furnished the power to move the mansion on 200 eight-inch rollers while cables eased the house down the ravine. A thirty-foot bridge was constructed to cross San Mateo Creek. At the end of two months the mansion had moved only 350 yards.

Tragically, the house caught fire shortly after its journey and lost two of its four stories, but remains standing today. Lindgren remodeled the house and finally occupied his "free" mansion that had cost him so much money and effort.

With the Swiss Chalet out of the picture, C. Templeton Crocker turned to Willis J. Polk, the well known architect of Filoli. Polk designed Uplands along neo-Classic, Renaissance palace lines, with the accent on "palace." With the experience of the earthquake still fresh in his mind, Polk built what is probably the most solid grand mansion on the Peninsula. Uplands utilizes steel, concrete, and brick to give the impression of great size.

In 1945, it enjoyed the distinction of being used by the Soviet Union as their residence while attending the San Francisco sessions to establish the United Nations.

In 1956 the Crystal Springs School for Girls acquired Uplands from the Crockers, and today the co-ed school, Uplands, continues to occupy the site at 400 Uplands Drive.

The second mansion of this era that remains today is Carolands at 565 Remillard Drive. Carolands was the dream house of Harriet Pullman, daughter of George Pullman and heir to the Pullman fortunes from parlor cars. Harriet married Francis J. Carolans of San Francisco in 1892. By 1912 they had acquired an expanse of land near the Burlingame Country Club. This original parcel was named Crossways.

Harriet was restless and desired more land and a magnificent house to reflect her wealth. In 1913 she purchased an additional 554 acres and employed a French architectural firm to design a 92 room chateau. For the garden design, Harriet sought out Achilles Duchene, a well known landscape architect.

Each room reflected their French influence, with two rooms transported in total from France. The gardens dazzled visitors with terraces and orchids. Over 32,000 trees and scrubs were planted to recreate the French Renaissance. The *piece de resistance* was the Temple of Love, which was copied after the structure at the Palace of Versailles.

Shortly after moving into their dream mansion, the Carolans discovered the flaws in the building's design. The French doors rattled in the Pacific winds and the numerous drafty French chimneys scattered ashes in every room. Even the French plumbing groaned throughout the home. After seven miserable months, Harriet Pullman Carolan moved to the East Coast and her husband retreated to Crossways Farm.

Late in the 1920s Harriet Pullman once again occupied the drafty French chateau, this time with her new husband. With the building's problems unresolved, she finally left Carolands, removed the furniture and put the property on the market.

Carolands was subdivided several times, but the chateau remained unoccupied until the 1950s when it was finally purchased and restoration begun. Once again, the mansion is occupied and a glimmer of hope appears on the horizon that current plans will restore Carolands to its rightful place among the mansions of Hillsborough.

Church of St. Matthew

SAN MATEO

The Episcopal Church of St. Matthew, San Mateo stands as a token of survivorship. The original church structure was completed in 1865 when San Mateo was merely a glimmer in the future city's eye.

The Howard family's estate overshadowed the small community, which consisted of a blacksmith's shop, a school, and new train station. There were no more than 150 people in the area. Despite the smallness of the community, the Howards donated a portion of their estate for the church. The style was Gothic and soon ivy covered the structure.

The parish worshiped in this small church until the 1906 earthquake destroyed the building. The Reverend Neptune Blood William Galwey led his parishioners to begin rebuilding at once. The architect of the hour, Willis J. Polk, happened to be a member of the parish and was enlisted to design a new church. Polk recalled the Gothic design of the original St. Matthew's in the new rendering and produced the masterful structure on the old site at El Camino Real and Baldwin Avenue.

The random-coursed Ashlar sandstone that covers this English Gothic church symbolizes the lifestyle of the parishioner.

Willis Polk used a steel frame with reinforced concrete to insure survival through any future earthquakes. This mighty structure was faced with gray Colusa sandstone laid in a random pattern which conveys a relaxed country style more in keeping with the community. The new church was quickly completed and consecrated in May, 1910.

Forty years after completion of the church, this sturdy construction was put to the test when the parish commissioned Milton T. Pflueger to enlarge the sanctuary. He successfully cut the church in half and moved the front end of the nave 30 feet west. The surviving nature of Polk's original structure allowed this move without any plaster cracking or a window breaking.

Willis Polk called upon his genius to produce a church structure to withstand the rigors of earthquake and moves. With a steel frame to match the parish's will, the Church looks forward to another century of expansion.

Central Park

SAN MATEO

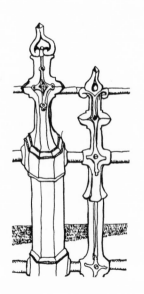

A detail of the wrought iron fence that rings Central Park.

Central Park in San Mateo brings the cool of tall trees in summer and the lure of games and sports in the fall. Once the estate and home of Captain William H. Kohl, this retreat from busy El Camino Real serves the community as an outdoor sanctuary from the stresses of a modern city.

The laughter of playing children has replaced the whispered conversations of women at tea. No longer do the ladies stroll beneath these stately trees, spin their parasols, and bend to admire the flowers. But the paths, gardens, and lawns remain the same; just the players have changed.

In 1874 Captain Kohl enclosed this estate with the wrought iron fence and garnished the entrance with the imposing stone gates on El Camino Real. The Kohl family purchased this retreat after the captain's successful years in the Alaska fur trade. Among the first commuters on the Peninsula, Kohl boarded the train each day to conduct his business in San Francisco.

After his death, the San Mateo estate was offered to the city whose citizens passed a bond issue to purchase the property. San Mateo Junior College occupied the old home from 1923 to 1927; in the latter years classes began to overflow into tents on the property. With overcrowded conditions, the college moved to new quarters and the mansion was demolished.

In Central Park, happy memories linger along the paths and under the towering trees. Calm and serene moments fill every corner of the park's Japanese garden. Large golden carp gulp at the green surface, bamboo rus-

An Asian flavor may be experienced as you enter the gates of the Japanese Garden in Central Park.

tle a whispered phrase, wading stones invite tiptoeing across the water, and the calm of the Orient envelops the visitor.

For livelier action, take a look at the playing field or enjoy a fast-paced game of tennis. Picnic tables and barbecue pits are available near the corner of Ninth Street and El Camino Real. On summer Sunday afternoons, the park reverberates with outdoor entertainment. On rainy winter days, the recreation center holds exercise groups and community gatherings.

For fast-paced or unhurried times, Central Park invites the passerby to enter through Kohl's stone gate and leave behind the cares of a modern city.

One of several stone gate pillars and wrought iron fencing surrounding Central Park.

Borel Estate

Sunshine Cottage in San Mateo was the last remaining building to be removed, but today in its place stands Borel Bank.

After three generations of prominence, the Borel Estate has disappeared. Covered by the Arthur Younger Freeway and an upscale shopping center, the home, gardens, and cottages no longer exist. "Gone but not forgotten," sings the refrain. The thread of the story begins with the discovery of gold in California when the merchant family of Borel became attracted to San Francisco.

When Alfred Borel returned to his native Switzerland from the California Gold Rush, his younger brother was ready for adventure and the fulfillment of a childhood dream. But, little did Antoine know that this would be the beginning of a long and productive life in San Francisco and San Mateo.

In the early fall of 1861, the two brothers boarded the *Great Eastern* bound for Boston and the family business in San Francisco. Three months after their journey began, they arrived in San Francisco.

Antoine joined his brother in business at Alfred Borel and Company, shippers and bankers. Within a few years Antoine had mastered the intricacies of boomtown banking and his brother longed to return to Switzerland. So at the age of 27, Antoine Borel became the sole manager of the business.

Under his hand the business prospered and grew with the growth of the Bay Area. The original name was maintained for many years but was eventually changed to Antoine Borel and Company.

In addition to managing his own business, Antoine had numerous connections in San Mateo County. His generous spirit combined with business acumen gathered praise from all his associates. He served as Consul for Switzerland for forty years and sat as a director of both the Bank of California and Wells Fargo Bank. Locally, he was associated with the San Mateo County Improvement Company, Park Development and the Spring Valley Water Company.

By the 1870s Borel had acquired a large tract of land in San Mateo. The property extended from El Camino Real to the foothills running along what

440 Montgomery Street in San Francisco's financial district was headquarters for the shipping and banking business of Antoine Borel and Company.

is today the Arthur Younger Freeway. In this attractive setting Antoine Borel and his wife, Grace, built their country home and raised their six children. By 1906 Antoine Borel, Sr. was spending more time in San Mateo while his only son, Antoine Borel, Jr., managed the San Francisco business.

The Borels developed their estate in San Mateo with a forest of trees surrounding neatly trimmed lawns that were dotted with grottos, ponds, and ornamental bridges. Winding throughout this wonderland were paths and drives. Horses were a passion with Borel and they grazed extensively into the hills. The property never served any commercial purpose but the community received generous gifts from the family.

Following a Swiss tradition, the Borel girls held an annual Christmas party for neighborhood children in the small Geneva Chapel at the edge of the estate. In the weeks preceding Christmas, local children were encouraged to write Santa Claus in care of the Borels. The Borel sisters endeavored to present each child with just what he wanted. Although differences in financial means separated the Borels from their neighbors, they were never aloof from the community.

Today, the tradition of the Borels sense of community continues with their banking presence in San Mateo. The Borel estate and gardens may be gone, but, indeed, they are not forgotten.

Twin Pines Mansion

BELMONT

Carl Janke established an amusement area in Belmont to entertain city folk from San Francisco who traveled by train to the wooded groves of Belmont. Their first impression was enhanced by the rail depot that opened in 1873.

Surrounding the station were gardens with a central fountain. The interior was partitioned into ladies' and gentlemen's parlors with dark cedar and redwood panels that heightened the sense of luxury.

From the Belmont Park station, carriages transported pleasure seekers to the Janke's park area at Sixth and Ralston Avenues. Here, under spreading oaks, buckeyes, and aromatic bay trees, Carl Janke developed a park based on a Hamburg *biergarten*. Janke provided generously for the revelers with a dance pavilion that held three hundred people. The attached pub contained a magnificent circular bar with a large keg of beer nestled in the center. A conical roof protected all these activities.

Janke's patrons always found amusement along the creek with paths and bridges crisscrossing the canyon. Children could ride the carousel and drink soda pop from the Janke Soda Works. Races and competitions attracted the attention of the crowds.

For most of the patrons, Belmont Park became an annual outing for good fun and a relief from the grime of the city.

Belmont thrived with the influx of patrons to the Janke's land. By the time of the great earthquake, the park had diminished and the 22 acres were sold to George Center. The Centers built a solidly constructed country home designed to withstand future rumblings of the earth.

111

Architecturally, Twin Pines Mansion demonstrates contrasts in style with a mix of the Mission revival in the red tile roof, curvilinear gable, and projecting eaves with exposed rafters. The interior is designed as an English country manor. The exterior walls are typical California Mission white stucco while the library is panelled in Douglas fir stained to resemble mahogany. The other rooms on the main floor exhibit this split personality with fine oak floors and ornate ceilings patterned after Renaissance gardens.

After the death of George Center, the estate was purchased by Dr. Vorbert Gottbrath, a San Francisco psychiatrist. He transformed the house into a hospital and within a few years Dr. William Rebec assumed management of the hospital. By this time Belmont had become a center for the treatment of mental illness, having four other sanitariums established in these wooded canyons. Strangely enough, the Ohlone Indians of the area considered this shady creek as a home for healing spirits.

Twin Pines Sanitarium continued as a treatment center for patients suffering from mental illness and alcoholism until 1975, when plans were proposed to develop the estate for office space and apartments. The citizens of Belmont rallied at the threat and passed the necessary bond issue to purchase the land and once again establish a park along the wooded creek.

Today the San Mateo Arts Council occupies Twin Pines Mansion with gallery space on the main floor and artist studios on the second floor. The former parlor, with its marble fireplace and plaster art ceiling acts as a perfect backdrop for local art shows. Visitors are welcome to browse and to observe the artists at work in their studios.

Once again in the summer time, Sunday afternoon concerts fill the canyon with music. The carousel and *biergarten* have disappeared but the spirit of a picnic in the park endures in Belmont.

The Mission Revival style of the George Center Mansion shows in the red tile roof, curved gable, projected eaves, and exposed rafters.

Ralston Mansion

BELMONT

Shrouded from public view by overgrown eucalyptus trees, the Ralston Mansion rises from the hillside along Ralston Avenue. The exterior design of the Peninsula's first grand mansion of the bonanza days defies definition. The lavish inner rooms bewilder the mind with their complexity and decoration.

William Chapman Ralston arrived on the Belmont scene in 1864 with the dynamic flourish of fame. Already a singular name as the founder of the Bank of California, Ralston proceeded to leave his mark on the Peninsula's future.

Shortly, after acquiring Count Leonetto Cipriani's land and home, he commissioned John P. Gaynor to revise and enlarge the modest structure begun under Cipriani's direction. Ralston approached the project with typical robust enthusiasm and flair. The resulting design incorporated his early years aboard the Mississippi riverboats with his complete devotion to promoting California. The woods for the interior came from California or were shipped from the Far East. The silver for the doorknobs and opera box railings came from the Comstock Lode. The resulting interior has been humorously called "Steamboat Gothic."

Actually, John P. Gaynor incorporated many revolutionary techniques that he later duplicated in San Francisco's Palace Hotel. One feature of the main floor called for the elimination of thresholds between the several rooms. The doors were in turn hung so that they could be raised out of sight or slipped into the wall. These conveniences allowed for the unimpeded flow of guests between the main floor rooms.

This grand mansion facade veils the interior beauty of a crystal palace, on the Notre Dame College campus.

115

The most spectacular feature of the central foyer is a second story opera box design with silver plated railings from which Mr. and Mrs. Ralston could view the arriving guests. Ralston enjoyed astounding dinner guests with a wall between the reception and dining rooms. This famous curtain wall never failed to evoke astonished remarks as it rose between two upper-floor walls to reveal the banquet table set with fine imported China, delicate linens, and crystal goblets.

Impeccable workmanship permitted these innovations and assisted the preservation of the mansion. The parquet floors incorporate mahogany, cedar, walnut, and maple with intricate designs that vary from room to room. Square-tipped wrought iron nails were forged and counter-sunk into the individual floorboards. Then the holes were plugged with matching wood pieces. Today these perfectly matched floor boards display a uniform surface without cracks or separation. Nine coats of enamel were used on the paneling. The care in craftsmanship ranks this house among the greatest in the state and country.

Ralston participated in the design and workmanship of the mansion. Most notably he contributed to the design of a ventilation system for the constant circulation of air throughout the mansion. An intricate system of louvers and lattice work under the roof brought air through ducts to each room, where the vents were covered with artistic metal work. Such ventilation was needed considering the size of Ralston's parties.

The *piece de resistance* of the Ralston Mansion remains the ballroom. Crystal chandeliers descend from the vented skylight to reflect their dazzling light in the mirrored walls. The elongated room evokes the memory of dancing couples with the women's billowing skirts floating across a flawless parquet floor. The room recalls the reign of the great riverboats on the Mississippi and Sacramento Rivers.

Ralston's empire of businesses, banking, and silver mines began to crumble after the panic of 1873. Within two years he was asked to resign from the Bank of California and on that same day he died while swimming in the San Francisco Bay. His partner, William Sharon, took possession of the estate and Ralston Hall continued as a center of peninsula social life.

In subsequent years the structure housed a finishing school and a mental hospital. In 1922, the Sisters of Notre Dame de Namur bought the estate for use as a four-year college. The sisters planned to move the College of Notre Dame from San Jose where it was established in 1851 as a two-year school and later became the first four-year women's college chartered by the State of California.

With diligence the sisters restored and refurbished Ralston Hall to its original glory. Today, the co-ed College of Notre Dame and its preparatory high school surround the building and the house has been declared both a state and national Landmark.

The main floor of Ralston Hall is available for social gatherings, community events, and weddings. Visitors are welcome to drive on campus and look at the outside of Ralston Hall. Tours of the interior provide explanations on the intricate details, and are available by appointment. Phone in advance (415) 593-1601.

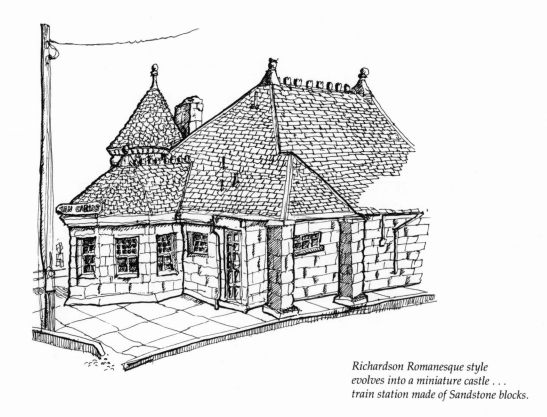

Richardson Romanesque style
evolves into a miniature castle . . .
train station made of Sandstone blocks.

San Carlos Railroad Depot

In the old days along the El Camino Real, dust rose in great clouds all summer long as carriages raced to beat the train to San Carlos. But, the station stood in Romanesque glory defying the dust to sully its exterior and waiting for the influx of new residents. From 1888 to the late 1920s the train depot waited for the rush of settlers that never came.

When Southern Pacific asked Nathaniel Brittan for an easement through his property for their tracks, he countered with a few requests of his own. He wanted a combination telegraph office, post office and depot, plus a lifetime pass for the train. Southern Pacific acquiesced to all his requests and through the help of Captain Nicholas Smith acquired some of the local sandstone used in the construction of the new Stanford University.

The depot design was grandiose for the simple dairy stop but local landholders' and railroad hopes ran high for the arrival of new property owners from the city. Real estate schemes in 1887 and again in 1907 failed miserably. The mop up operation of the last venture brought Fred Drake into San Carlos as a representative of Mercantile Trust of San Francisco. Drake had the business acumen and flair needed to turn the misadventures of others into success. In 1917, he established his real estate office directly opposite the train station and began a lifelong career dedicated to the growth of San Carlos.

In the long run, people settled in San Carlos and created the suburbs that Fred Drake had worked so hard to develop. The land boom is over in San Carlos and the suburbs are here to stay. And, in the midst of all this modern haste, the romantic rail station still conjures up the dreams of another time.

Nathaniel Brittan's Party House
SAN CARLOS

San Carlos in the 1870s was a rather tame spot for a world traveler, writer and *bon vivant*. Nathaniel Brittan was all of these things when he turned his eye to the construction of the manor at 40 Pine Street.

He knew change was on the way and granted Southern Pacific right of way through his land with the stipulation that the railroad build a combination post office, depot, and telegraph office on his property. With these modern conveniences even the most reclusive location could become livable for the world traveling lover of the good life.

With these accouterments in place, Brittan began construction of his wood, stucco and shingle home. He had the roof tiles imported from France and insisted on Victorian embellishments. He brought a certain flair to all his endeavors. Other colorful features included a bear pit, a flock of peacocks, a tea house and an automatic iron gate (the forerunner of the suburban garage door opener).

Most of these innovations have disappeared but the most outstanding addition to the estate remains in place today. Brittan enjoyed a rousing party better than most of his contemporaries. On one traumatic night of revelry, Mrs. Brittan was forced to fire a shotgun over the heads of Brittan's riotous cronies to get their attention. To spare his family and his art collection, Brittan built a party house considerably removed from the main building.

Architecturally, the party house is a delight. The steeply gabled roof gives the impression of birds lightly descending from the sky. The octagonal struc-

A whimsical house with red-colored sideboards and soaring gables suggest a Christmas castle.

*The manor house at
40 Pine Street, San Carlos.*

ture is topped by a windowed cupola that increases this sensation of flight in motion. Admirably suited to the purpose, the house is constructed of durable redwood and contains a gaming room for billiards and other Victorian diversions for gentlemen.

The party house, located at 125 Dale Avenue, remains a visual diversion and delight. San Carlos has grown up around these digs. But, on a quiet summer evening, the laughter of Brittan's cronies seems to drift from the windows of the party house and reminds us that the true *bon vivant* lives on in our hearts.

County Courthouse
REDWOOD CITY

San Mateo County most likely holds the record for the number of courthouses destroyed by earthquake. Of the four dedicated in the city, two have been severely damaged by quakes. The present courthouse was barely completed when the 1906 earthquake struck and the dome, which was never structurally attached to any base, acted as an inverted pendulum to destroy the empty wings.

Although the supervisors had accepted the building, they had not met in their new quarters. The rebuilding of the structure was plagued with setbacks, redesign problems, and scandal. Finally, in 1910, the supervisors held their first meeting in their new home.

After these numerous delays and overpayment to the contractors, the final rendering cost the taxpayers three times the original estimate. But the richness of the long-awaited building mollified the citizenry and civic pride swelled under the magnificent dome.

Today, under a recently restored dome, the visitor captures this pride as the light plays through the stained glass of the rotunda onto the delicate mosaic floors. A grand stairway lined with finely crafted iron balustrades leads to the balcony second level. From this vantage point the dome sparkles like a crown jewel in green, gold and red. The second floor columns are in fake marble, a popular medium in the early part of this century.

With the 1986 restoration completed, this leading example of Roman Renaissance style in public architecture becomes a notable historical attrac-

*Below the dome,
the interior stairway
leads up to a
courtroom garnered
with Victorian
splendor.*

tion. Each piece of glass in the dome was removed during restoration for cleaning. The whole dome was reassembled with fresh solder and a modern support system. With these earthquake protection steps, the supervisors hope this courthouse can withstand the earth's next rumblings.

Next to the Courthouse stands a wooden structure that demonstrates the ability to endure earthquakes plus two site moves. The Lathrop House at 627 Hamilton Street is another hardy survivor. This excellent example of Steamboat Gothic was built in 1863 by Benjamin G. Lathrop, who served the county as its first clerk, recorder and assessor. The house was originally located at the present site of the now historic Art Deco Redwood Theatre on Broadway.

As a historical landmark and restored Victorian, the Lathrop House welcomes visitors on a regular schedule. For visitor information, call (415) 365-5564. Docents are available to answer questions and guide you through the house.

On the ground floor the kitchen is equipped with butter churn, wood burning stove, and oak table. The original pine floors and carefully duplicated Victorian wallpaper complete the historical picture. On the second floor, a child's bedroom with period dolls and the master bedroom with bath chamber seem taken from an early tintype.

Lathrop House is a showplace of domestic Victorian architecture while the County Courthouse and its restored dome display this architecture in the public sector.

Salt Loading Derrick
REDWOOD CITY

Arriving at San Francisco International Airport on a bright sunny day, the air traveler views the magenta and brown ponds of the South Bay's salt industry. The rusty acres of stagnant waters appear a far cry from the pure white salt of the dinner table.

Along the shores of Redwood City and the East Bay, thousands of shallow water acres comprise one of the world's greatest salt producing areas. These solar evaporation ponds require a special combination of climatic factors to yield world production figures. The dry climate coupled with vast marshy acreage continues to place Redwood City and the Leslie Salt Company among the top salt producers worldwide.

In the absence of marshes and mud flats, water birds use these evaporating ponds as their habitat. Snowy egrets, herons, and stilt-legged dowitchers inhabit the edges of the ponds.

By the turn of the century, San Mateo County offshore marshlands had become the center for the Bay Area salt industry. Several companies competed for control of the marshlands which they endeavored to level, dike and flush. Nearby railroad spurs encouraged the continued extension of solar ponds from San Mateo south to Redwood City.

Of these early companies, only Arthur Whitney's Leslie Salt Company in Redwood City remained after 1920. During the Great Depression, August Schilling assumed control of Leslie Salt and, upon his death, the new owners concentrated all operations in Redwood City. By the 1960s Leslie Salt owned

50,000 acres of salt ponds around the San Francisco Bay, making salt production one of the area's leading industries.

The glistening ponds and dinosaur derricks symbolize the growth of Redwood City industry and harbor facilities. Despite all this activity, the placid shore birds observe our hustle and watch the slow-drying salt ponds.

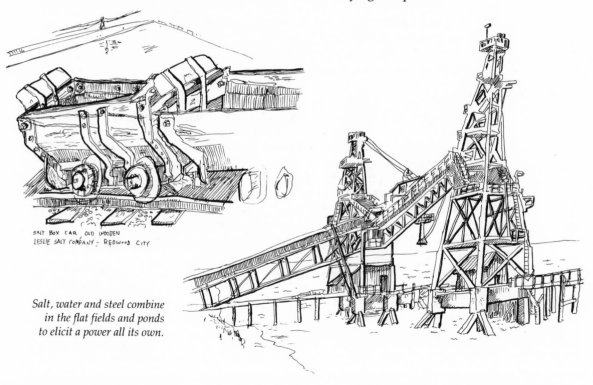

SALT BOX CAR OLD WOODEN
LESLIE SALT COMPANY - REDWOOD CITY

*Salt, water and steel combine
in the flat fields and ponds
to elicit a power all its own.*

Watkins-Cartan House

ATHERTON

Commodore James T. Watkins of the Pacific Mail Steamship Company moved his family from Maryland to California when the Gold Rush reached high gear. Fashionable South Park in San Francisco made an elegant winter home, but when the fogs of summer shrouded the city, the sea captain cast his eye for a more suitable residence. By 1863 regular train service extended down the Peninsula, enabling access to areas such as Atherton.

Within a few years, Commodore Watkins bought eighteen acres from the estate of his good friend Faxon Atherton. The parcel of land contained many large Valley Oaks and prompted the Watkins to name their estate Fair Oaks.

The home originally stood near the railroad and gave its name to the depot and road along the property's edge. In 1903, the building was moved to its present location. The trauma of this transfer and the 1906 earthquake did no damage to the fine building.

The sturdiness of the structure reflects the skill of ship carpenters. These carpenters reinforced the house with a crisscrossed sheath between the inner and outer walls.

The house presents a vertical impression with steeply pitched roofs and dormers, but the flattened arches on the wide veranda soften this effect. Tucked into the peak of each gable is a round window, giving the effect of a small Gothic rose window in the nave of a church.

The clean lines of the house are enhanced by a circular drive with a sweep of lawn in the foreground. Four palm trees recall the vertical lines of the

A Victorian Gothic with a pristine quality, the Watkins-Cartan house, built in 1866, is one of the oldest houses in the Menlo Park-Atherton area.

Queen Anne Victorian on Selby Lane, depicts country grandeur.

dormers, presenting a unified picture of house and landscape.

At the edge of the garden the branches of pine, mulberry, live oak, and magnolia trees soften this Gothic Revival house. The total picture transports the observer to the years following the discovery of gold in California.

To see the Watkins-Cartan House take El Camino Real north past Glenwood Avenue and Menlo College to Isabella Avenue which is the first left after the campus. This charming reminder of the past is at 25 Isabella Avenue.

For a further look at nineteenth century California, Atherton has established a local park incorporating some buildings from the period. Holbrook-Palmer Park is located nearby on Watkins Avenue between El Camino Real and Middlefield Road.

This town park is a good stop for a picnic on the rolling lawn in front of the Victorian water tower or a chance for the children to explore the playground. Originally, this 22-acre site was purchased by Charles Holbrook as a summer residence and named the ''Elmwood'' after his native state of New Hampshire. The home continued in the family as a summer residence until 1958, when the property was willed to the Town of Atherton.

The town, along with a foundation board, administer the park and develop funds for an active community center. The park is open daily with the restored main house available for special events. For information and schedules call the Park Director (415) 324-4521.

As the Atherton town line meanders through the mature oaks and palms, many former mansion sites fall within the boundaries of Menlo Park. The Payne-Douglass mansion, once the home of Leon F. Douglass, is now the administration building for the Menlo School. This magnificent example of a Baroque Period mansion with classical touches is located on Valparaiso Street and was built in 1910 for Mrs. Theodore Payne. In 1921 Leon Douglass, the inventor, bought the home and immediately installed his workshop in

Water tower in Holbrook-Palmer Park.

131

the basement. He was a prolific inventor and his experiments resulted in many twentieth century innovations. Most notable was the Victrola with the recognizable symbol of the floppy-eared dog listening to "His Master's Voice."

Church of the Nativity

MENLO PARK

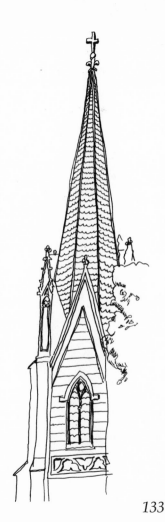

Peaceful and serene, the Church of the Nativity resides in a circle of green grass and trees on Oak Grove Avenue. This Catholic Church, built in the 1870s, reflects the loving care of the parish and demonstrates the features of a typical Victorian Gothic Church.

The elegant lancet windows are used throughout the structure, except for the lovely rose window over the altar which was donated in 1900. The tower spire is flanked by finials and their knobby, mushroom-like decorations called "crockets". Over the front entrance wood craftsmen have carefully designed trefoil decorations by first cutting a triangle then using a jigsaw to complete the clovers. At every turn the church speaks volumes on attention to detail, love and care.

The smell of incense lingers ever so faintly and the dark wood of the pews blends with the rosewood hammerbeam trusses. Each pew row has a small door that closes inconspicuously for Victorian decorum. The stained glass windows glow with rich red cloaks and green garment cloths. On the wall of the nave a ship's clock breaks the silence with its rhythmical ticks.

The Church of the Nativity beckons the passing visitor to enter and rest for awhile. It is located on Oak Grove Avenue just off busy Middlefield Road.

The Church of the Nativity holds a very special place in the parish hearts. In the 1950s, the population growth prompted talk of replacing this venerable structure with a modern design. The parishioners resisted all suggestions and held firm to retain their beloved Gothic Revival sanctuary.

Camp Fremont

WORLD WAR I

During World War I, Menlo Park received thousands of recruits into Camp Fremont. Today a tiny park marks the location of the headquarters at the southwest corner of Santa Cruz and University Avenues. Forty-two thousand young men came from California and the Midwest to train for ''The War to End All War.''

The size and population of the camp dwarfed nearby Menlo Park, whose businesses and contractors reaped the benefits of the military base. Tents and wooden headquarters buildings covered 1300 acres of leased land. Camp Fremont served as one of 16 training centers nationwide and became as self-sufficient as possible with two million dollars in expenditures for streets, gas, electricity, water, a theater, library, hospital and post office.

In 1919, after the end of the war, the U.S. Government moved quickly to dismantle Camp Fremont. They cancelled their leases and demolished many of the wooden buildings. Some of these wooden relics continue their existence in the Menlo Park area, one of which now contains a popular tavern, The Oasis, on El Camino Real near Partridge Avenue.

This typical World War I building was moved to the El Camino Real location and raised one floor. False columns and denticulated trim were used to hide the joining.

A closer look at the upper level and roof reminds the viewer of the Great War. You can almost see the doughboys leaning from the windows with their hats set at a jaunty angle.

Who would ever guess that this building had been through a World War?

Inside The Oasis, a pub atmosphere overwhelms the senses. Heavily carved tables dominate the room with edges worn thin by decades of elbows. Initials of former Stanford students cover the walls of each booth. This tavern can become a busy place, serving drinks and hamburgers to crowds of young people. Closer to the Stanford campus and lightyears from this tavern atmosphere, stands another Camp Fremont building. This second building, the former camp Hostess House, contains the MacArthur Park Restaurant at 27 University Avenue in Palo Alto.

During World War I the military asked the Young Women's Christian Association to build and staff Hostess Houses at each military training center. These facilities provided an appropriate setting for soldiers to meet with their wives, friends and relatives. At Camp Fremont, the Y.W.C.A. constructed the Hostess House on Santa Cruz Avenue at the current site of the Menlo Park Presbyterian Church.

The outstanding feature of this recreation facility was its design by Julia Morgan, the architect of Hearst Castle at San Simeon. By the outbreak of the war, Morgan had come to national prominence as an architect. Born and raised in the Bay Area, she was the first woman in 1894 to earn a Bachelor of Science degree in civil engineering at the University of California.

With this educational background, Morgan regarded architecture as the fine art of mechanics and worked with the Y.W.C.A.'s basic budget to produce a graceful building unlike most Army projects of the period. The ordinary materials of board and batten took on a charmed life under her creative hand.

When Camp Fremont closed, the Y.W.C.A donated the Hostess House to Palo Alto for use as a community center, the first in the country. As such, the center became a grand living room for the city, with the doors open from morning to late evening. Concerts and lectures were scheduled and a child care center established.

In time, the popular program demanded larger quarters and the Julia Morgan structure became the Veterans' Memorial Building. No major architectural changes occurred during these busy years and even today, as a popular restaurant, much of Morgan's original design remains visible.

Another reminder of these World War I days is the Menlo Park Railroad Station. Although originally built in 1867 as a small three room station, the demands of a wartime population required the addition of a waiting shed on the northern end of the station.

From the earliest days, the ladies' waiting room occupied the southeast end of the building and provided a decorative touch with a polygonal window. Leland Stanford, one of the "Big Four" in railroad development, was a regular user of this tiny station and by 1890, some renovation was deemed necessary.

A rectangular bay addition with five windows was constructed under the trackside gable. Double doors provided access to the main waiting room. The resulting structure demonstrates all the popular styles in architecture at the turn of the century—Victorian Gothic, Queen Anne, and Stick-Eastlake.

Of equal interest is the Gatehouse in the Menlo Park Civic Center at 439 Ravenswood Avenue. This wellkept Victorian gatehouse once served as the entrance to the William E. Barron estate and was built in 1863. This great estate covered a vast area—from San Francisquito Creek to Ravenswood Avenue in a broad strip from the El Camino Real to Middlefield Road. The now lost grand manor was built in the late 1800s for Milton S. Latham, railroad magnate, a former Governor of California, and former U.S. Senator.

Today, the mansard-roofed gatehouse serves as offices for the Junior League and can be rented for receptions and small gatherings. For information and fees contact the Menlo Park Recreation Department at (415) 858-3470.

Saint Patrick's Seminary

Garden Court interior at the seminary.

As you turn off Middlefield Road into St. Patrick's Seminary grounds, you enter a tunnel of towering trees and massive oleanders. This drive slows your progress with speed bumps but the roughness disappears as you behold the brick facade of the seminary. The palm trees that were mere bushes at the seminary's opening now stand as giant shade providers in the center of the broad circular drive.

St. Patrick's stands as a tribute to the long held dream and careful planning of San Francisco's second Archbishop, Patrick W. Riordan. In the 1890s, this dynamic archbishop foresaw an imminent shortage of parish priests for the burgeoning churches of the archdiocese. The pool of Irish and European priests was dwindling without a western seminary to replenish the supply.

Kate Johnson, a Catholic, responded to the need by donating 86 acres of her property for the new seminary. The officials of the archdiocese found the climate mild and the location secluded with magnificent scenery.

On August 24, 1898, Archbishop Riordan, assisted by two bishops and more than 100 priests, gathered to dedicate the almost completed seminary building. Designed by Charles I. Devlin, the Romanesque style of architecture was chosen to insure light, spaciousness, and comfort. Quiet tones of red brick with stone trim were selected for the exterior. The original building boasted a 225-foot-high square central tower topped with a cross. This 37-foot-square tower was flanked by two wings with plans for a large chapel that would complete the secluded seminary garden. All of the furniture was constructed of polished oak to insure comfort with dignity and reserve.

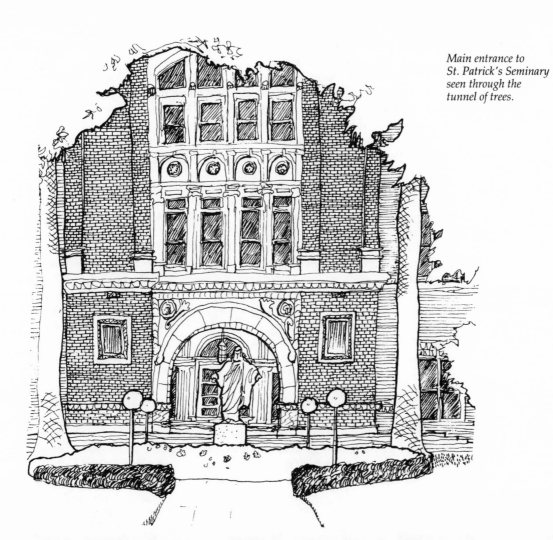

*Main entrance to
St. Patrick's Seminary
seen through the
tunnel of trees.*

139

Originally built with four stories, today's structure reflects the modifications made after the 1906 earthquake. This massive quake toppled the tower, destroyed the upper story, and crumbled the incomplete chapel.

The resources of the archdiocese were stretched to capacity with tremendous losses in every parish. In restructuring the building, the angled roof and upper story were removed along with the tower.

When St. Patrick's Seminary opened in 1898, Archbishop Riordan brought five priests from the Society of St. Sulpice as the first faculty to 31 students. This French order dedicates their service exclusively to train young men as parish priests. At that time, St. Patrick's student body ranged from high school and college to graduate theological students. Tuition was $250 per year and the days were long in accordance with Sulpician tradition.

As late as the 1950s, seminarians remained on the seminary grounds (except when they returned home for vacations). Due to the rigors of study and prayer many young men left before completing their training. It was not unusual for a class of fifty students to ordain only seven or eight of that number.

Today, the seminarians enjoy a more relaxed atmosphere without the regulations calling for black cassocks and Roman collars. These young men join the ranks of distinguished graduates, which include one cardinal, seven archbishops, and more than 20 bishops.

St. Patrick's Seminary is open for visitors Mondays through Fridays from 9:00 a.m. to 3:00 p.m. Enter through the main door on the circular drive. The information desk is located just inside the entrance. The grand staircase leading to the second floor dominates the entrance hall. The entrance to the chapel is located between these grand oak stairways.

The chapel is designed for seminary use with polished oak stalls lining the long walls. The sunlight fractures into multiple colors as it passes through stained glass windows which depict scenes from Christ's Passion and Crucifixion. The sanctuary light flickers in the ruby glass container near the altar.

Within these thick walls, removed from the speeding traffic of Middlefield Road, a few moments of reflection can capture the dedication of the faculty and students of St. Patrick's Seminary.

In the area behind St. Patrick's Seminary, the largest Victorian country house of the Menlo Park-Atherton area remains in use. Today, this grand building of Italianate design houses the Peninsula School on Peninsula Way near Berkeley Avenue. Originally built in 1882 for James V. Coleman, nephew of William O'Brien of Comstock fame, the stark white mansion rises like a grand wedding cake from the landscape. Cast iron ornamentation creates the illusion of a storybook house.

Some tragic overtones surround the early history of this house. Before they were able to occupy their home, Coleman's young wife died. Although he retained ownership of the house and visited the estate regularly, local lore insists that he never set foot inside the home. In 1906, the San Francisco Archdiocese purchased the estate and used it as part of St. Patrick's Seminary. In 1925, the present owners, the Peninsula School, purchased the mansion and renovated the interior for classroom use. Today, the house remains a feast for the eyes as a reminder of a young couple's dream.

If the trees and grasses of this area have captured your heart, then a picnic in Flood Park, which is located on Bay Road between Marsh Road and Ringwood Avenue, would make an excellent stop. Once part of the Flood Estate, this park is famous for its large native oak and bay trees. Facilities include tennis courts, a softball diamond, a baseball field, a young children's play area, barbecue, and picnic areas and extensive lawns.

There is an entrance fee for each car and reservations are not necessary for family picnics. However, for large group activities call (415) 363-4021 at least ten days prior to your planned event. There are no reservations on holidays. For additional information about the facilities and regulations call the ranger at Flood Park, (415) 363-4022.

142

Garden Court of the Allied Arts Guild, Menlo Park.

Allied Arts Guild

MENLO PARK

Menlo Park's Allied Arts Guild formed in the 1920s as a center for craftsmen and artists to create their works in a peaceful community with the mutual support of their colleagues. Artist Pedro de Lemos and architect Gardner Dailey created an ambience in the Spanish Colonial Revival style. Their delicate rendering transports the visitor to the halcyon days of the American Arts and Crafts Movement.

In the early days of its development, the center attracted workers in pottery, wrought iron, glass, and fiber-arts. In 1929, Mr. and Mrs. Garfield Merner purchased this three-acre site to establish the crafts guild along European lines. Pedro de Lemos directed the importing of tiles, art objects, and decorative stones from Spain. The iron craftsmen designed the lamps and wrought iron plates that cover each light switch in the main dining hall. Tucked away in corners, special Spanish wall pieces carry out the architectural design.

In the gift shop, the exposed beams are decorated with delicate designs and each bolt has an ornate iron cap. These Spanish accents appear in the courtyard fountain and on the massive stone jars along the brick walls. The murals and frescos were created by Maxine Albro and members of the de Lemos family. The paths are paved with stones from the San Francisquito stream, which forms the boundary between Santa Clara and San Mateo counties.

The spirit of Allied Arts resides in the dedicated volunteers who serve lunch and afternoon tea in the Allied Arts Guild Tea Room to support the Children's Hospital at Stanford. The familiar blue smock distinguishes these volunteers from the visitors that they greet and help with selections in the Traditional Shop.

Allied Arts has become a holiday tradition, and each Christmas season Peninsula residents come to see the Christmas tree and browse through the many small decorated shops. In summer the gardens glow with color and emit the tranquil sound of splashing fountains. Demonstrations of handcrafts and weaving are a regular part of the center's schedule of activities.

To visit the Allied Arts Guild take the University Avenue exit on Highway 101 to El Camino Real. Go north on El Camino Real until Cambridge Avenue and turn left, then follow the signs to the Guild on Arbor Road. Lunch is served by the volunteers Monday through Friday with a buffet style luncheon on Saturdays. The complex of shops and demonstrations is open from 9:30 a.m. to 5:00 p.m. everyday except Sundays. For information phone (415) 324-2588.

Another tradition in Menlo Park is the publishing headquarters of Sunset Magazine and Sunset Books. The seven-acre site at the corner of Middlefield and Willow Roads was once part of the Rancho de las Pulgas, a land holding that resulted from an 1815 land grant to Don Jose Arguello. The adobe style buildings reflect this Spanish origin and were designed by Cliff May for Sunset Magazine in 1962.

Sunset Magazine was founded in 1898 by Southern Pacific Railroad to promote the growing West. In 1928, Laurence W. Lane purchased the magazine and continued the exclusive promotion of the essence of Western living. At headquarters, ideas are tested in the gardens and specially designed kitchens.

Guided tours of these facilities are available on working days, both in the morning and afternoon. Visitors are welcome to enjoy the Thomas Church landscaped gardens and lawn areas during office hours.

A heavy oak door swung open within the thick adobe walls of Sunset Magazine headquarters in Menlo Park.

144

The high ceiling of the main entrance hall captures the open spirit of the West and the glass wall facing the gardens brings a view of the Pacific Coast plantings indoors. A mature California Live Oak dominates the planned garden that takes the visitor on a tour of Pacific Coast regions, flaunting specimens such as rhododendrons of the Northwest and cacti of Southern California. The Allied Arts Guild and the Sunset Magazine headquarters combine to offer visitors to Menlo Park a memorable morning or afternoon. For a taste of California, these centers offer the visitor an exceptional opportunity to celebrate San Mateo County's long tradition of hospitality.

It's hard to believe that the Menlo Park
Train Station is the oldest in continuous
use in the state of California. It was built in 1867.

145

Additional Places to Visit

THE COASTLINE

BRODERICK-TERRY DUEL SITE in Daly City at Lake Merced Boulevard and Northgate Avenue, is located in a small park. Historic marker tells the story of this famous duel in 1859. The park makes an excellent picnic stop.

SAN PEDRO VALLEY COUNTY PARK located at the eastern end of Linda Mar Boulevard past the Sanchez Adobe. Steelhead spawning grounds are within the parks boundaries. Steelhead come here in December–January and again in March–April. Visitor Center with self guided nature trail, picnic areas and hiking trails.

MOSS BEACH AND FITZGERALD MARINE RESERVE combine to make the finest place on the coast to become acquainted with tidal pool ecology. The reserve has a small picnic area for a wonderful rest stop along Highway 1. At Moss Beach drive west on California Street to reach this picnic area.

POMPANIO BEACH on Highway 1 south of San Gregorio Beach has been named for a lone Indian who made a last desperate stand against the Spanish settlers. Here a fine sand beach stretches below the bluffs of the coast and is considered by some photographers as a perfect picture stop. A few protected picnic tables make this an excellent place for lunch.

BUTANO STATE PARK is south of Pescadero and five miles east of Highway 1 on Cloverdale Road. From Highway 1 take Pescadero Road through the town of Pescadero to Cloverdale Road and turn south on Cloverdale. This state park is rugged and contains backpacking areas under first growth redwoods. The lower elevations display a rain forest environment with a profusion of ferns. For camping reservations call (415) 879-0173.

THE HIGHLANDS

ROD McLELLAN COMPANY, 1450 El Camino Real, is just off Interstate 280 in South San Francisco. Take the Hickey Boulevard exit east to El Camino Real and turn south to the "Acres of Orchids." Indeed, there are acres of greenhouses sheltering every imaginable type of orchid. This world famous orchid grower is open to the public every day of the year, except major holidays, from 8:00 a.m. to 5:00 p.m. Free tours are offered daily at 10:30 a.m. and again at 1:30 p.m. For groups of five or more, please call ahead for a reservation — (415) 871-5655.

JUNIPERO SERRA PARK is adjacent to the cities of San Bruno and Millbrae on Crystal Springs Road. The most direct route to the park is from El Camino Real in San Bruno by going west on Crystal Springs Avenue for one mile to the park entrance. Live Oak Nature Trail introduces the visitor to this park which provides excellent views of the bay and San Francisco International Airport. At the highest point in the park there are picnic tables and barbecue pits nestled under a grove of eucalyptus trees.

EDGEWOOD COUNTY PARK is located east of Interstate 280 and along Edgewood Road. In springtime this serpentine ridge supports a magnificent wildflower display. You can enjoy gold fields, tidy tips, lupines, poppies and many more flowers tucked into the serpentine outcroppings.

MEMORIAL PARK is the oldest in the San Mateo County Park system. This area provides an outstanding opportunity to view virgin redwoods. Also available are picnic areas, family campsites, a visitor center, a creek swimming area, group areas, and hiking trails. Take Highway 84 or Highway 1 to Pescadero Road.

PORTOLA STATE PARK contains 52 drive-in camping spaces and a backpacking camp with six sites just three miles from the parking area. This mixed hardwood forest offers excellent hiking opportunities plus the short self-guided Sequoia Nature Trail. Take Alpine Road from Skyline Boulevard to reach this park. This drive is one of the most beautiful on the peninsula. For information call (415) 948-9098. For camp reservations call (800) 444-7275

147

THE BAYSHORE

ORANGE MEMORIAL PARK in South San Francisco offers 21 acres of parkland in the heart of the city. This park which is located at Orange and Tennis Avenues features covered picnic tables, an outdoor barbecue, children's play area, tennis courts, par course and an indoor swimming pool.

SAN MATEO COUNTY HISTORICAL ASSOCIATION MUSEUM maintains permanent exhibits that reflect the cultural history of the county from the earliest Native American residents through the Age of Elegance. The Museum offers guided tours to groups without charge. The museum is located on the San Mateo College Campus at 1700 West Hillsdale Boulevard. They are open Mondays through Thursdays from 9:30 a.m. to 4:30 p.m. and Sundays from 12:30 p.m. to 4:30 p.m. Closed Fridays and Saturdays. For further information, call (415) 574-6441.

SAN MATEO FISHING PIER is a portion of the old San Mateo Bridge. Fishing in the quiet waters of the bay can be a rewarding experience. Take Highway 101 to East Hillsdale Boulevard, east to Beach Park Boulevard in Foster City.

CONGRESSMAN LEO J. RYAN MEMORIAL PARK commemorates the congressman's tragic death on November 18, 1978, when he and his companions were gunned down on the airstrip near Jonestown, Guyana. This park enjoys a peaceful setting on Central Lagoon in Foster City. Located at Hillsdale Boulevard and Shell Avenue, this park offers picnic tables, tennis, a senior par course, and a regular par course with views of wind surfers skimming the lagoon.

UNITED STATES GEOLOGICAL SURVEY at 345 Middlefield Road, Menlo Park offers for sale in their bookstore topographical maps for any area on the peninsula, in California or the Western United States. Other maps that are available show mineral resources and earthquake fault zones. A complete catalog of maps produced by the U. S. Geological Survey is also sold here. The lobby area contains a permanent display on the history of map making. The bookstore is open only on weekdays during regular business hours. For further information call (415) 853-8300.

Additional Reading

Foster, Lee, *Making the Most of the Peninsula*, Palo Alto: Tioga Publishing, 1989.

Hynding, Alan, *From Frontier to Suburb: The Story of the San Mateo Peninsula*. Belmont: Star Publishing Co., 1982.

Olmsted, Roger R., *Here Today: San Francisco's Architectural Heritage*, San Francisco: Chronicle Books, 1968.

La Peninsula, San Mateo County Historical Association Journal, 1700 West Hillsdale Blvd., San Mateo, CA 94402.

Morrall, June, *Half Moon Bay Memories*. El Granada: Moonbeam Press, 1978.

Postel, Mitchell P., *Peninsula Portrait: A Pictorial History of San Mateo County*, Windsor Press, 1988.

Regnery, Dorothy F., *An Enduring Heritage: The Architectural History of the San Francisco Peninsula*, Stanford: Stanford University Press, 1976.

Stanger, Frank M., *Sawmills in the Redwoods: Logging on the San Francisco Peninsula, 1849–1967*. San Mateo: San Mateo County Historical Association, 1967.

Stanger, Frank M., *South From San Francisco*. San Mateo: San Mateo Historical Society, 1963.

Wagner, Jack R., *The Last Whistle: Ocean Shore Railroad*. Berkeley: Howell-North Books, 1974.

Ken Paul

Ken Paul is uniquely qualified to give us this book. A native to San Francisco, Ken studied at the California College of Arts and Crafts, in addition to earning a B.A. at Simpson College and an M.A. in art and education from the University of Hawaii. Combining an interest in art with historic preservation, Ken has been sketching buildings on the Peninsula for quite a few years. In cooperation with the San Mateo County Office of Education, he produced *History in Print*, a book designed to teach local history through art. His prints have been shown at numerous exhibits, including those at the San Mateo County Arts Council gallery in Belmont and the San Mateo County Historical Museum at the College of San Mateo.

Alexandra Gautraud

Alexandra Gautraud is an experienced history and travel writer whose articles have appeared in magazines and newspapers. Alexandra grew up in New York City before graduating from Albertus Magnus College in New Haven, Connecticut. After moving to the Bay Area, she received her master's degree from the University of San Francisco. She has served on the faculties at the College of Marin and Santa Rosa Junior College. Currently, as adjunct faculty, Alexandra teaches graduate students in writing for publication at the University of San Francisco. She is editor of The Oakland Museum's *History Guild News* and a member of the Bay Area Travel Writer's Group.

Glossary

Architectural Terms

Arcade A series of arches supported by columns or piers.

Ashlar A squared or dressed rectangle of stone for facing walls.

Balustrade A series of upright, often vase-shaped supports for a rail.

Belfry A tower from which bells are hung within.

Chandelier A lighting fixture with branches usually hanging from a ceiling.

Crockets The shape of stylized leaves that decorate the edges of spires.

Cupola A small dome on a circular base crowning a roof.

Dormers The roof structure of a vertically set window on a sloping roof.

Double-hung Windows A window with two sashes, one above the other, arranged to slide vertically past each other.

Fanlight A semicircular window with radiating members set over a door or window.

Finial An ornament at the top of a spire.

Flume An artificial channel conveying water for industrial use.

French doors Two adjoining doors that have glass panes from top to bottom and are hinged at opposite sides of the wall.

Gable A triangular decorative feature, such as that over a door or window.

Gargoyles Grotesque spouts projecting from the gutter of a building to carry water clear of the wall.

Lancet Windows A narrow pointed arch window.

Louvers Any of a series of sloping slats set in an opening to provide air and light but to shed rainwater outward.

Maltese Cross One of the most ancient symbolic and ornamental devices.

Mosaic The process of making designs by inlaying small bits of colored stone or glass in mortar.

Outhouse An outdoor small shelter containing a toilet.

Parquet Flooring of thin hardwood laid in patterns on a wood subfloor and highly polished.

Quoin Units of simulated stones at the corner of buildings.

Rose Window A circular window with patterned tracery arranged like the spokes of a wheel.

Rotunda A round building, hall, or room, especially one with a dome.

Spire Anything that tapers to a point, as a pointed tower or steeple.

Transom A horizontal bar of stone or wood across the opening of a window or across a panel.

Trefoil Any ornamental figure resembling a threefold cloverleaf.

Trestle A framework of vertical or slanting uprights and crosspieces, supporting a large horizontal structure.

Tuscan One of the simplest classical orders characterized by unfluted columns with a ringlike capital and a Doric-like frieze.

Veranda A roofed open gallery or porch.

Architectural Styles

Arts and Crafts In America the Green brothers, Charles and Henry, were the leaders of the style. The emphasis was natural wood, stone and burned bricks, along with low-pitched roofs, welcoming entrances with comfortable verandas and balconies.

Baroque A style characterized by much ornamentation and curved rather than straight lines.

Carpenter Gothic The emphasis is steep roofs, ornamented verandas, and steep central gables decorated with Gothic motifs.

Classical Revival A synergestic style suggested by the Beaux Arts, 1880-1920.

Edwardian A style characteristic of the first three English Kings named Edwards, (1272-1377 AD). In America this style was popular in the 1920s.

Georgian This style emphasized rigid symmetry, elaborate entrances geometrically proportioned, hipped roofs and sash windows.

Gothic Recognized by the use of pointed arches used over doors and windows and interior vaulting.

Greek Revival Buildings are noted for a gabled portico or temple facade with columns in the Doric or Ionic Order. Its roof slope is low and weighted with parapets and large cornices in a Post and Beam type construction.

Mission Revival Mission-shaped dormers or roof parapets with red tile roof coverings depicted this style, along with wide overhanging eaves and a porch roof supported by square piers. A smooth stucco surface covers the exterior walls.

Queen Anne Victorian This style shows a wide variety of verandas and balconies, turrets and towers, as well as materials of wood and stone.

Richardson Romanesque A unique style that features a heaviness on the horizontal approach with a rough texture. There are massive stones used to emphasize solidity and permanence of the structure. The window reveals are deep, door openings cavernous and accented with short, robust columns. Towers create a massive and bold outline flanked by "eyebrow" dormers, broad round arches and carved intertwining floral details.

Romanesque A style characterized by the used of round arches and vaults, thick, massive walls and interior bays.

Roman Revival Characteristic of the style are a projecting central pediment, a classical portico, symmetrical facade, and a shallow dome. The arch and dome are the main features of this style.

Saltbox Characteristics of this style are a roof with a lean-to appearance, heavy oak-timber frames, a massive central chimney, heavy doors, and small high leaded casement windows.

Spanish Colonial Revival Characteristics of this style are a one story building with low-pitched or flat roof with parapet, red tiled roof, arcaded porches, adobe brick construction with a stucco covering and a walled garden.

Steamboat Gothic A variation of Gothic Revival used in an eclectic style with a steamboat construction design on parts of the interior.

Proper Names

Alcalde (Spanish) The mayor of a Mexican-American town,

Ohlones (Spanish) A word used by the Spanish in California to name one of the Indian groups in San Mateo County called the *Olxan*. Another name for the Indians is *Costanoan*, Spanish word for coast people).